Empire and Papacy—

Random House Historical Pamphlet Edition

GENERAL EDITORS:

BRIAN TIERNEY

DONALD KAGAN

L. PEARCE WILLIAMS

Empire and Papacy— A Search for Right Order in the World?

Random House

Third Edition

987654321

Copyright © 1967, 1972, 1976,
1977 by Random House, Inc.

Library of Congress Cataloging in Publication Data
Main entry under title:
Empire and Papacy—A Search for Right Order in the World?
  (Random House Historical Pamphlet Edition; 5)
    Reprint of a section of the 3rd ed. of Great Issues in
Western Civilization edited by B. Tierney, D. Kagan, and
L. P. Williams.
    1. Church and state—History—Addresses, essays, lectures.
2. Papacy—History—To 1309—Addresses, essays, lectures.
3. Middle Ages—History—Addresses, essays, lectures.
I. Series: Great Issues in Western Civilization; 5.
CB245.G68 1977 no. 5 [BV631] 909'.09'821s
ISBN 0-394-32053-0 [322'.1'094] 76-49011

Manufactured in the United States of America

Acknowledgments

(Page numbers for articles in this text appear before each acknowledgment.)

P. 9 "Annals of Lorsch," from *Monumenta Germainiae Historiae, Scriptores,* G. H. Pertz, ed. (1826), p. 38. Trans. by B. Tierney.

P. 10 "Frankish Royal Annals," from *Monumenta Germainiae Historiae, Scriptores,* p. 188.

P. 10 Einhard, *Life of Charlemagne,* trans. by S. E. Turner (1880), pp. 65–66.

P. 10 From *Life of Leo III (Vita Leonis III),* in *Le Liber Pontificalis,* L. Duchesne, ed. (1892), pp. 6–8. Reprinted by permission of Editions E. de Boccard. Trans. by B. Tierney.

P. 12 Francis Ganshoff, *The Imperial Coronation of Charlemagne* (1949), pp. 13–28. Reprinted by permission of the author.

P. 14 Walter Ullmann, *A Short History of the Papacy in the Middle Ages* (1972), pp. 81–84. Reprinted by permission of Metheun and Co. Ltd.

P. 17 Brian Tierney and Sidney Painter, "From Reform to Revolution," in *Western Europe in the Middle Ages, 300–1474,* 3rd ed., (1974), pp. 193–195. Copyright © 1970, 1974 by Alfred A. Knopf, Inc. Reprinted by permission of Alfred A. Knopf, Inc.

P. 19 "Decree Against Lay Investiture," from E. F. Henderson, *Select Historical Documents of the Middle Ages* (1892), p. 365. Reprinted by permission of G. Bell & Sons Ltd.

P. 19 "Dictatus Papae," from S. Z. Ehler and J. B. Morrall, *Church and State Through the Centuries* (1954), pp. 43–44. © Burns & Oates, 1954. Reprinted by permission.

P. 20 "Henry IV's Letter to Gregory VII, 1076," from T. E. Mommsen and K. F. Morrison, *Imperial Lives and Letters of the Eleventh Century* (1962), pp. 150–151. Reprinted by permission of Columbia University Press.

P. 22 "Deposition of Henry IV, 1076," from E. Emerton, *The Correspondence of Pope Gregory VII* (1932), pp. 90–91. Reprinted by permission of Columbia University Press.

P. 23 "Gregory VII's Letter to the German Princes," from *The Correspondence of Pope Gregory VII,* pp. 111–112. (Columbia Univ. Press)

P. 24 "Second Deposition of Henry IV, 1080," from *The Correspondence of Pope Gregory VII,* pp. 149–152. (Columbia Univ. Press)

P. 26 "Gregory VII's Letter to Hermann of Metz, 1081," from *The Correspondence of Pope Gregory VII,* pp. 166–175. (Columbia Univ. Press)

P. 29 "Concordat of Worms," from S. Z. Ehler and J. B. Morrall, *Church and State Through the Centuries* (1954), pp. 48–49.

P. 30/P. 52 Phillip Hughes, *A History of the Church* (1935), Vol. 2, pp. 224–228/ pp. 390–392, 394. Copyright 1935, Sheed & Ward, Inc. Reprinted by permission of Sheed & Ward, Inc., and Sheed & Ward Ltd., London.

P. 31 Geoffery Barraclough, *Origins of Modern Germany* (1946), pp. 118–120. Reprinted by permission of Basil Blackwell & Mott Ltd., London.

P. 32 Gerd Tellenbach, *Church, State, and Christian Society at the Time of the Investiture Controversy,* trans. by R. F. Bennett (1940). Reprinted by permission of Humanities Press and Basil Blackwell & Mott Ltd., London.

P. 36 "Sermons on the Consecration of a Pontiff," from J. P. Migne, ed., *Patrologica Latina* (Paris: 1855), Vol. 217, cols. 657–658, 665. Trans. by B. Tierney.

P. 37 "The Decretals," from Brian Tierney, *The Crisis of Church and State, 1050–1300 with selected documents* (1964), pp. 133–138. © 1964. Reprinted by permission of Prentice-Hall, Inc., Englewood Cliffs, N.J.

P. 41 Albert Hauck, *Kirchengeschichte Deutschlands,* from *Innocent III, Vicar of Christ or Lord of the World?* trans. by J. M. Powell (1963), Vol. 4, pp. 2–3. Reprinted by permission of James M. Powell.

P. 42 R. W. Carlyle and A. J. Carlyle, *A History of Medieval Political Theory in the West* (1909), Vol. 2, pp. 217–222. Reprinted by permission of William Blackwood & Sons Ltd.

P. 46 "Frederick II: A Contemporary View," from G. G. Coulton, *St. Francis to Dante* (1906), pp. 242–243, David Nutt, London.

P. 47 "Deposition of the Emperor, 1245," from S. Z. Ehler and J. B. Morrall, *Church and State Through the Centuries,* pp. 81, 86.

P. 48 "Frederick's Reply," from Brian Tierney, *The Crisis of Church and State,* pp. 145–146. (Prentice-Hall)

P. 50 "A Defense of the Deposition," from Brian Tierney, *The Crisis of Church and State,* pp. 147–149. (Prentice-Hall)

P. 54 A. L. Smith, *Church and State in the Middle Ages* (1913), pp. 226–227, 233, Clarendon Press.

Preface

A major purpose of this series of pamphlets is to convince students in Western civilization courses that the essential task of a historian is not to collect dead facts but to confront live issues. The issues are alive because they arise out of the tensions that men have to face in every generation—tensions between freedom and authority, between reason and faith, between human free will and all the impersonal circumstances that help to shape our lives.

In order to achieve any sophisticated understanding of such matters, students need to read the views of great modern historians as they are set out in their own words. Students need to develop a measure of critical historical insight by comparing these often conflicting views with the source material on which they are based. They need above all to concern themselves with the great issues that have shaped the course of Western civilization and not with historical "problems" that are mere artificially contrived conundrums.

We believe that there are three major themes whose development and interplay have shaped the distinctive characteristics that set Western civilization apart from the other great historic cultures. They are the growth of a tradition of rational scientific inquiry, the persistence of a tension between Judaeo-Christian religious ideals and social realities, and the emergence of constitutional forms of government. These three themes are introduced in the first pamphlets of the series. Readers will find them recurring in new forms and changing contexts throughout the rest of the pamphlets. We hope that in studying them they will come to a richer understanding of the heritage of Western civilization—and of the historian's approach to it.

BRIAN TIERNEY
DONALD KAGAN
L. PEARCE WILLIAMS

Empire and Papacy—

CONTENTS

QUESTIONS FOR STUDY

1 *How does Einhard's account of the coronation of Charlemagne differ from the other accounts? How can the discrepancy be explained?*

2 *Who do you think took the initiative in planning Charlemagne's coronation?*

3 *Why was the issue of "lay investiture" so important in the eleventh century?*

4 *Is it correct to call Gregory VII a "revolutionary"? If so, why? If not, why not?*

5 *How did Gregory VII defend his deposition of Henry IV? How could a supporter of the king have replied to the pope's arguments?*

6 *After reading Innocent III's letters, which account of his position do you find more convincing, that of Hauck or that of the Carlyles?*

7 *Why did Innocent IV quarrel with Frederick II? Was the pope justified in deposing the emperor?*

During the period 800–1250, two great themes dominated the institutional history of the Western world. One was the growth of feudal institutions and the slow building of national monarchies on a feudal basis. The other was a prolonged struggle between popes and emperors for the leadership of Christian society.

The line of Roman emperors in the West became extinct when the puppet emperor Romulus Augustulus was deposed in 476. The medieval empire was created when Pope Leo III crowned Charlemagne as emperor in St. Peter's Church on Christmas Day, 800. It was a new kind of empire. The old Roman Empire had been essentially a Mediterranean state with its greatest centers of wealth and population in the East. The new empire was created by an alliance between the papacy and the Germanic peoples north of the Alps. The alliance was formed when the Frankish leader Pepin seized the throne of the Franks in 750. Pope Zachary approved of his action and the pope's legate, St. Boniface, crowned and annointed Pepin as king. Pepin in return invaded Italy, conquered the lands around Rome, and bestowed them on the papacy. This was the beginning of the temporal sovereignty of the popes over central Italy, the founding of a papal state that would last down to the nineteenth century.

By 800 Pepin's son, Charlemagne, had made himself ruler of a vast kingdom including France, Germany, and northern Italy. In that year Pope Leo III was expelled from Rome by a local revolution, and he took refuge with Charlemagne. Charlemagne occupied Rome and reinstated the pope. Leo then took a public oath declaring himself innocent of the charges that had been made against him by his enemies, and this was accepted in place of a formal trial. A few days later, the pope crowned Charlemagne in St. Peter's "as the king rose from praying" and the people acclaimed him as emperor. According to one account, Charlemagne was surprised by the pope's action. Historians have never been able to agree on whether the initiative in creating a new empire in the West came from the pope or the Frankish court (pp. 340–344). In any case the event was literally epoch making in its significance. Charlemagne's empire disintegrated soon after his death, but the imperial title was revived by the German king Otto the Great, who was crowned as emperor at Rome in 962. From then onward the title of "Roman Emperor" gave the German kings a claim to rule Italy as well as Germany.

The early emperors saw themselves as representatives of God on earth, divinely appointed to govern religious as well as secular affairs. Otto I made a regular policy of using bishops and abbots as officers of the royal government. He endowed the greater prelates with vast estates and with rights of secular government over them. They then formed a useful counterpoise to the power of the secular nobility. The lay princes often held their positions by hereditary right; the prelates were chosen and appointed entirely at the will of the king. Naturally, he looked for loyal and efficient servants of the monarchy in making his *choices. The emperor himself installed a new bishop in his see by "investing" him with ring and staff, symbols of spiritual office.*

In an age when divine-right monarchy seemed the only alternative to total chaos, the emperors' theocratic claims were generally accepted and, indeed, enthusiastically supported by the clergy. The ninth and tenth centuries were a difficult time for the church. In many parts of Europe ecclesiastical lands fell under the control of the local feudal nobility. The lord of a village as a matter of course appointed the village priest. More ambitious nobles set themselves up as "protectors" of a local abbey. In practice they would seize the revenues of the abbey and assume the right to appoint its head —probably one of their own relatives or servants. Some bishoprics similarly fell under secular control. We read of churches let out as fiefs to illiterate nobles and of bishoprics being bought and sold for hard cash. The old discipline of the Western church, which prescribed celibacy for priests, was forgotten or ignored. Married priests and bishops bequeathed their churches to their heirs like pieces of private property. Pastoral duties were neglected. Even the papacy fell under the control of the brigand nobility of Rome. Some monasteries survived as centers of dedicated Christian life. Those of the order of Cluny (founded in 910) were especially influential. But by the beginning of the eleventh century there was desperate need for a more general reform of the church as a whole.

King Henry III (1039–1056) was a zealous church reformer. In the early years of his reign he asserted his authority over the unruly nobility of Germany, and he stood at the height of his power as an unchallenged theocratic monarch when he journeyed to Rome for his imperial coronation in 1046. In Rome Henry undertook the considerable task of reforming the papacy itself. Ironically, it was this initiative of the emperor that led to all the subsequent struggles of papacy and empire. So long as Henry lived, the pope worked for the moral reform of the church throughout Europe in harmony with him. But, after Henry's death, the reformers in Rome became convinced that the subordination of churches to laymen—including kings—was the root cause of all the church evils that they were trying to abolish. In 1075 Pope Gregory VII denounced the practice of "lay investiture"—the conferral of spiritual office by laymen. When King Henry IV of Germany refused to obey the pope's decree, Gregory excommunicated him and deposed him from his office of kingship (pp. 348–350). This was the first occasion when a pope claimed to depose a king. It raised many difficult problems. According to Gregory VII, spiritual offices were not to be subject to laymen. Were temporal rulerships to be subject to an all-powerful priesthood?

The investiture dispute has often been seen as a turning point in Western history. The church asserted its independence of the state, and, in the name of reform, the leaders of the church sought to impose a radically new order on Christian society. The dispute itself ended in a compromise (p. 357). But the problem of the right relationship between spiritual and temporal power remained to be worked out in subsequent struggles between the popes and the next great dynasty of German kings, the Hohenstaufen.

Between 1150 and 1250 the underlying problem was a political one. The kings of Germany were determined to establish an effective rule over Italy, but the popes were determined to maintain their political autonomy in the papal states. The two powers, it seemed, could not exist side by side. One had to be superior to the other. More and more overtly, the popes began to assert that, since they were vicars of Christ, all power on earth was given to them—power to control emperors and kings as well as bishops and priests.

Pope Innocent III (1198–1216) is widely regarded as the greatest exponent of the ideas and ideals introduced into the church during the Gregorian reform movement. He combined an intense concern for the moral reform of the church with a conviction that the pope should be the supreme arbiter of all the affairs of Christian society. He was a more sophisticated thinker than Gregory VII and a more adroit diplomat. His writings provide both exalted, generalized statements about papal power and closely reasoned arguments justifying his right to intervene authoritatively in the political disputes of Europe (pp. 364–369). Innocent was fortunate in that, when he came to the throne, the powerful emperor Henry VI had just died and two candidates, Philip and Otto, were contending for the imperial throne. Innocent III threw his support to Otto, who was duly crowned as emperor in 1209. But when Otto attacked the papal lands in Italy, Innocent excommunicated him and transferred his support to Frederick, the young son of the former emperor Henry VI. A year later, Frederick was accepted as king by the German princes. In 1220, four years after Innocent's death, he was crowned emperor by the next pope, Honorius III.

In favoring Frederick II, Innocent III for once made an error of judgment. The young prince grew into a formidable monarch. Moreover, he inherited the throne of Sicily from his mother and so had a legitimate claim to rule all Italy, north and south. Frederick devoted all his energy to building a consolidated, centralized monarchy in Italy. The popes feared that in such a state they would be reduced to playing the role of mere imperial court chaplains, and they bitterly opposed Frederick's plans. In particular, Innocent IV (1243–1254) used every spiritual and temporal re-

source of the papacy in order to thwart Frederick's ambitions. The cities of Lombardy, rich, proud, eager for independence, joined the pope in the struggle against the emperor. In the end Frederick died with Italy still unsubdued. His son and grandson also died within four years, and the line of Hohenstaufen emperors came to an end. The German princes emerged as autonomous rulers in their own states. Innocent IV had destroyed the medieval empire as an effective unit of government. Some historians maintain that he also destroyed the moral prestige of the papacy by his single-minded concentration on worldly politics. Others see him as a high-spirited defender of the liberties of the church.

The outcome of the controversy affected the whole future structure of Western institutions. Germany and Italy remained disunited until the nineteenth century. The popes established themselves as effective heads and rulers over the whole Western church. But they did not make good the claim to be theocratic monarchs ruling over the temporal as well as the spiritual affairs of Europe. The destruction of imperial authority merely facilitated the rise of nation states, which, in the end, proved more formidable adversaries of the papacy than the medieval empire had been. Western society emerged from the conflict of empire and papacy with an inbuilt dualism, a certain tension between church and state that has persisted down to the present. Finally, the claim of the church to resist secular rulers in the name of a higher law was of major importance in the growth of constitutional restraints on monarchy. "To that conflict of four hundred years," wrote Lord Acton, "we owe the rise of civil liberty."

1 *The Founding of the Medieval Empire*

The first three of the following accounts are by Frankish writers. The fourth is by a member of the papal court.

FROM *Annals of Lorsch*

800

IN THE SUMMER Charles gathered together his lords and faithful men in the city of Mainz. When he saw that there was peace throughout his dominions he called to mind the injuries that the Romans had inflicted on Pope Leo and, setting his face toward Rome, he journeyed there. After his arrival he summoned a great council of bishops and abbots, together with priests, deacons, counts and other Christian people. Those who wished to condemn the apostle Leo came before this assembly. When the king realised that they did not want to condemn the pope for the sake of justice but maliciously, it became clear to the most pious prince Charles and to all the bishops and holy fathers present that, if the pope wished it and requested it, he ought to clear himself, not by judgment of the council, but spontaneously, by his own will; and this was done. When the pope had taken the oath, the holy bishops, together with the clergy and prince Charles and the devoted Christian people, began the hymn, *Te Deum laudamus, te Dominum confitemur.* When this was finished the king and all the faithful people with him gave thanks to God who had preserved the apostle Leo sound in body and mind. And he passed the Winter in Rome.

Now since the title of emperor had become extinct among the Greeks and a woman claimed the imperial authority it seemed to the apostle Leo and to all the holy fathers who were present at the council and to the rest of the Christian people that Charles, king of the Franks, ought to be named emperor, for he held Rome itself where the Caesars were always wont to reside and also other cities in Italy, Gaul, and Germany. Since almighty God had put all these places in his power it seemed to them that, with the help of God, and in accordance with the request of all the Christian people, he should hold this title. King Charles did not wish to refuse their petition, and, humbly submitting himself to God and to the petition of all the Christian priests and people, he accepted the title of emperor on the day of the nativity of our Lord Jesus Christ and was consecrated by the lord Pope Leo.

FROM *Frankish Royal Annals*

801

ON THE MOST HOLY DAY [*the chronicler reckons December 25 as the first day of the new year—Ed.*] of the nativity of the Lord, as the king rose from praying at Mass before the tomb of the blessed apostle Peter, Pope Leo placed a crown on his head and all the Roman people cried out, "To Charles Augustus, crowned by God, great and peace-giving emperor of the Romans, life and victory." And after the laudation he was adored by the pope in the manner of the ancient princes and, the title of patrician being set aside, he was called emperor and Augustus. A few days later he commanded the men who had deposed the pope the year before to be brought before him. They were examined according to Roman law on a charge of treason and condemned to death. However, the pope interceded for them with the emperor and they were spared in life and limb. Subsequently they were sent into exile for so great a crime.

FROM *Life of Charlemagne* BY *Einhard*

THE ROMANS HAD INFLICTED many injuries upon the Pontiff Leo, tearing out his eyes and cutting out his tongue, so that he had been
Nov. 24, 800   compelled to call upon the King for help. Charles accordingly went to Rome, to set in order the affairs of the Church, which were in great confusion, and passed
Dec. 25, 800   the whole winter there. It was then that he received the titles of Emperor and Augustus, to which he at first had such an aversion that he declared that he would not have set foot in the Church the day that they were conferred, although it was a great feastday, if he could have foreseen the design of the Pope. He bore very patiently with the jealousy which the Roman emperors showed upon his assuming these titles, for they took this step very ill; and by dint of frequent embassies and letters, in which he addressed them as brothers, he made their haughtiness yield to his magnanimity, a quality in which he was unquestionably much their superior.

FROM *Life of Leo III*

THE FAITHFUL ENVOYS OF Charlemagne who had returned with the pope to Rome . . . spent more than a week examining those most evil malefactors to discover what crimes they could impute to the pope. Neither Pascal nor Campulus nor their followers found anything to say against him; so the aforementioned envoys seized them and sent them to France.

After a time the great king joined them in the basilica of the blessed apostle Peter and was received with great honor. He called together a council of archbishops, bishops, abbots and of all the Frankish and Roman nobility. The great king and likewise the most blessed pontiff took their seats and made the most holy archbishops and abbots seat themselves while all the other priests and the Frankish and Roman nobles remained standing. This council was to investigate all the charges that had been made against the holy pontiff. When all the archbishops, bishops and abbots heard this they declared unanimously, "We do not dare to judge the apostolic see which is the head of all the churches of God, for we are all judged by it and its vicar, but it may be judged by no one according to ancient custom. Whatever the supreme pontiff decrees we will obey canonically." The venerable pontiff said, "I follow the footsteps of the pontiffs who were my predecessors. I am ready to clear myself of the false charges that have been basely made against me."

On a later day, in the same church of the blessed apostle Peter, when all were present, namely the archbishops, bishops, abbots, all the Franks who were in the service of the great king and all the Romans, the venerable pontiff mounted to the altar holding the four Gospels of Christ and in a clear voice declared under oath, "I have no knowledge of these false crimes which the Romans who have persecuted me have basely charged me with, nor any knowledge of having done such things." When this was done all the archbishops, bishops, abbots, and all the clergy chanted litanies and gave praise to God and to our lady the ever-virgin Mary, Mother of God, and to the blessed apostle Peter, prince of the apostles and of all the saints of God.

After this, on the day of the nativity of our Lord Jesus Christ, all were again gathered together in the basilica of the blessed apostle Peter. And then the venerable holy pontiff with his own hands crowned Charles with a most precious crown. Then all the faithful Romans, seeing how he loved the holy Roman church and its vicar and how he defended them, cried out with one voice by the will of God and of St. Peter, the key-bearer of the kingdom of Heaven, "To Charles, most pious Augustus, crowned by God, great and peace-giving emperor, life and victory." This was proclaimed three times before the tomb of blessed Peter the apostle, with the invocation of many saints, and he was instituted by all as the emperor of the Romans. Then on that same day of the nativity of our Lord Jesus Christ the most holy bishop and pontiff anointed Charlemagne's most excellent son, Charles, as king, with holy oil.

Historians have differed in their interpretations of the events leading up to the imperial coronation. Francis Ganshof held that the coronaton was planned at the Frankish court.

FROM *The Imperial Coronation of Charlemagne*
BY *Francis Ganshof*

IT SEEMS TO ME that in order to understand Charlemagne's accession to the imperial dignity, we must go back to Alcuin's chief concern. The famous abbot of Saint-Martin de Tours, whose intimacy of thought with his royal protector is well known, was between 796 and 799 full of anxiety concerning the Church. The storm caused by the conflict about the worshipping of the sacred images had only just calmed down; abuses dishonoured the clergy; in Saxony resistance to Christianity was still active; hesitations and misunderstandings threatened to imperil the evangelisation of the Danubian countries and above all the adoptionist heresy preached by Elipand of Toledo and Felix of Urgel was gravely menacing the purity of faith in the West.

In May 799 arrived the news of the criminal attempts against pope Leo III: to Alcuin, deeply devoted to the Holy See, it was the scandal of scandals.

As has been noticed, it is in the midst of these anxious days that, about the year 798, the expression *Imperium Christianum*—"the Christian empire"—appears in Alcuin's correspondence; it was frequently used by him up to 801/802. He used it when writing to Charlemagne and to his friend Arn, archbishop of Salzburg.

That "Christian empire" is the whole of the territories submitted to Charlemagne's authority and inhabited by the *populus christianus,* which is the community of Christians spiritually dependent on Rome. Charles's task is to govern, defend and enlarge it and closely linked with these obligations is his duty to protect Faith and Church. It is in the letters where he most insistently implores Charlemagne to take measures against the adoptionist heresy or to re-establish the pope in his authority, that Alcuin uses these expressions.

It seems to me quite unquestionable that we are here in the presence of an obvious indication.

Charles is master of almost the whole Western Christendom and Rome itself is subject to his protectorate. He is more than a king; his states form a whole which may well deserve to be qualified "empire": the underlying idea is that Charlemagne must be emperor.

When Alcuin begs him to interfere in favour of Leo III he shows him the Holy See humiliated, the imperial throne in Byzantium vacant, and he proclaims that on Charles, the king of the Franks, chief of the "christian folk," rests the safeguarding of the Church's highest interests.

That character of guardian of the faith, protector of the church, was precisely the one which ecclesiastical tradition attributed—indeed quite arbitrarily—to the Roman emperor; Gregory the Great, in whose writings Alcuin had been steeped, is categorical in this respect. In the eyes of Alcuin it appeared a necessity for the sake of the Church that there should be an emperor, successor of the Christian Roman emperors, who would end the scandals and above all prevent new ones.

If Alcuin has expressed these ideas with particular force, he certainly was not the only one to think as he did. It would be strange if Arn, one of his most faithful correspondents, had had no notion of the kind. We have reason to believe that another of his correspondents, Angilbert, abbot of Saint-Riquier and familiar of Charlemagne as well as declared lover of one of his daughters, shared the same ideas.

*   *   *

Did Alcuin and the other "imperialists" succeed in convincing Charlemagne of their views? It certainly was a hard task. In the first place because other duties may have appeared to him more urgent than to go to Rome in order to settle the affairs of the papacy. It was difficult also because Charlemagne seems to have been prejudiced against the imperial title; he might even have felt some aversion from it. Finally because Charlemagne, in spite of his appetite for learning, lacked intellectual culture and most likely did not thoroughly grasp what Alcuin and his people meant by the imperial dignity—a notion which required some slight knowledge of history and theology, even if unsophisticated, and some capacity of abstraction.

And yet Charlemagne decided to go the way that, according to me, had been pointed to him.

*   *   *

How did things happen in Rome?

The pope whom Charlemagne had re-established on his throne was surrounded by enemies and soon was compelled to clear himself publicly of the accusations brought forward against him. He was but a toy in the hands of the Frankish king and of his counsellors. He would certainly not have been in a position to oppose the realisation of a scheme which Charlemagne had adopted. His interests moreover were quite different: he might well believe that an emperor would efficiently protect him, and besides, he had always been compliant towards Charles. He might also have found pleasure in removing any suggestion of ·subordination to Byzantium. One must admit that Leo III showed himself quite willing to take his share in the events.

The leading part belongs, according to me, to a few Frankish clerics of the royal circle, namely, I take it, to Arn and to Alcuin's confidential agents, whom he had sent to Rome: Whitto-Candidus, Fridugisus-Nathanael and other monks of Saint-Martin de Tours. Thanks to their interference, the ideals of Alcuin and of the other "imperialist clerics" won the day.

They sat together in the council with other ecclesiastics; Frankish, Lombard and Roman. There were very strenuous debates, which resulted in the oath on which on December 23rd the pope justified himself. After this on the same day, the council and "the whole christian folk"—that is to say, the Franks and the Lombards as well as the Romans—decided that Charlemagne must be made emperor. Was not the imperial throne occupied by a criminal woman, vacant? Were not Rome—capital of the Caesars—Italy, Gaul and Germany in his possession? Charlemagne accepted.

The imperial dignity for Western Europe had been restored in his favour on that very day.

There only remained the ceremony at which this was to be celebrated.

On December 25th at St. Peter's according to the rules that were known in Rome, but which the king and the Franks ignored and did not care about, Charles was regularly elected by the "Roman people" expressing their will by the way of ritual acclamations. But before these had sounded, the pope had himself crowned the new emperor. Like many weak characters, Leo III had played a crooked game. Through his gesture which could be understood as a symbolic livery— as a *traditio*—he had given the impression that it was he who had invested Charlemagne with the imperial dignity.

There lies, in my opinion, the reason of the great displeasure shown by Charlemagne, the reason for which he hesitated during several months to adorn himself with the imperial title in his diplomas and for which he refused to adopt the one which had appeared in the acclamations: *imperator Romanorum.*

He did not wish to seem as if he held his empire from the pope and especially not from a pope who owed him so much and had taken him now by a kind of treachery. When in the palace church of Aachen, on September 11th, 813, he himself crowned his son Louis emperor— or perhaps ordered him to take the crown from the altar and to put it on his head—without any interference of either pope or clergy, he showed how to his liking things should have taken place on December 25th, 800.

Walter Ullmann maintained that Pope Leo took the initiative in order to free the Roman church once and for all from control by the East Roman emperors at Constantinople.

FROM *A Short History of the Papacy in the Middle Ages*
    By *Walter Ullmann*

BECAUSE CHARLEMAGNE'S abiding aim was to be in the West what the emperor was in the East, a similarity of his government to that exercised by the emperor necessarily emerged. Not only in the government proper, but also in some peripheral matters the resemblance was rather close. When the pope, Leo III, had considerable difficulties with the local Romans in 798–9, he undertook the arduous journey to Paderborn in Germany to implore the patrician of the Romans to render him help in Rome.

On the occasion of this visit he became acquainted with the building programme which engaged Charlemagne's attention at this time, that is, the building of the palace at Aachen to which contemporaries had somewhat ominously referred as 'The Second Rome'. Uncomfortable memories of 'New Rome' must have crossed the pope's mind, especially when he further learned that next to the minster envisaged there was to be 'a sacred palace' for the king himself and another building, called 'The Lateran', was expressly designated 'the house of the pontiff'—all this could not but evoke and provoke comparisons with Constantinople and the imperial régime. What this building programme signified was a transfer of Rome to Aachen, where the pope's role might well have to be reduced to the level of that generally allocated to the patriarch of Constantinople, the domestic imperial chaplain. Although Charlemagne did undertake the campaign to liberate Leo III from the hostile clutches of the Roman population, the pope himself took the initiative in a different direction. There is no warrant for saying that Charlemagne had Leo III formally tried. What in actual fact happened was that at a large meeting of high ecclesiastics, Frankish magnates and other high-placed laymen in St Peter's basilica, the accusations raised against the pope by the Romans were discussed at great length, but the pope upon a solemn oath denied all the crimes and charges. The reason why the pope took this oath, was the unanimous endorsement which the whole meeting gave to the ancient, but hitherto never applied principle that the pope could not be judged by anyone. . . .

It was the first time that this principle had been invoked. The significance of this invocation can hardly be exaggerated. In his function as pope and as successor of St Peter he stood above the law. The application of the principle was historically and, from the papal point of view, governmentally far more important than the events to which it led. It was also this meeting which on 23 December 800 decided that Charlemagne, the king of the Franks, should be called emperor. And Charlemagne agreed to this suggestion in all humility, as the contemporary record has it. For according to contemporary views the throne at Constantinople was vacant, because a woman, Irene, ruled there.

The understanding of the subsequent events presupposes the proper assessment of this point in conjunction with the deep Frankish veneration for St Peter and the somewhat unpalatable impressions that the pope had received on inspecting the building projects at Paderborn. In any case, Charlemagne was indisputably the acknowledged Ruler of Europe between the Pyrenees and the Elbe, and without exaggeration could be spoken of as the Ruler of the West as far as this had been opened up. That all these circumstances and facts were easily capable of being turned to the advantage of the papacy, was a conclusion which the extremely alert, realistic and perceptive Leo III quickly reached. It was he who seized the initiative. Thereby he continued the dynamic lead which had characterized the actions of the papacy during the last decades. And as subsequent history was to show, as long as the papacy kept the initiative in its own hands, and thus utilized the emerging constellation of circumstances in the service of its programme, its success was generally assured.

*   *   *

Since in 800 the throne in Constantinople was considered 'vacant' and since everything else indicated that the situation was propitious for papal initiative, Leo III in accordance with a concerted plan acted during Christmas Mass. That Charlemagne had readily agreed to 'accept the name of emperor' only two days earlier, was no doubt a particularly weighty circumstance. Leo III celebrated Christmas Mass, not in the expected church (in Santa Maria Maggiore) but in St Peter's —the very place held in the highest esteem by the Franks. During this service the pope put a 'most precious crown' on the head of Charlemagne just as he was rising from his kneeling position, whereupon the assembled crowd shouted the acclamation in a prearranged manner, so that now (to quote the most reliable source) 'he was set up as Emperor of the Romans'. It was the meaning that was given to the 'coronation' by the crowd at St Peter's which took Charles somewhat aback, for the role he had accepted was that of an emperor, but not that of an 'Emperor of the Romans'. This embodied a very special function. The emperor of the Romans was in fact the one in Constantinople, the historic successor of the ancient Roman emperor, who as such inherited the claim to universality of his Rulership. But this was not the function which Charlemagne wished to play. To be an 'emperor' was no more than a streamlined king who ruled over several nations, and it was this role which he had agreed to accept before Christmas. Clearly there was a wide gulf between papal and Caroline views. For if Charles had accepted the function of a universal Ruler as represented in the fully-fledged Roman emperor, the consequence would have been—as was certainly intended by the papacy—that the empire in the East would have been considered to have ceased to exist as a legitimate Roman empire, and that Charles himself would have now been the 'true' emperor of the Romans. His intention, on the contrary, was to be in the West what the emperor was in the East. His aim was parity or co-existence with the empire in the East.

2 The "Investiture Contest"

In 1046 the Emperor Henry III established a line of re-forming popes at Rome. The following reading describes how the Roman reformers turned against the imperial authority after Henry's death.

From Reform to Revolution

THE EMPEROR HENRY III died in 1056, leaving an infant son, Henry IV, to succeed him. During the long minority of this young prince, the first signs of dissatisfaction with the imperial authority began to appear among the reformers at Rome, and soon their dissatisfaction turned to bitter hostility. To understand the issues involved in the ensuing conflict, we must recall the way in which the imperial government was organized in mid-eleventh century. Henry III gave great temporal power and wealth to his bishops, but he chose them himself and used them as royal servants. Their support was essential to the stability of his government. Similar conditions existed to a lesser degree in France and England. There was little idea of any separation between the spheres of spiritual and temporal government. Kings appointed bishops, but bishops ruled secular provinces. A kingdom was a sort of unified church-state over which the king presided. Royal appointment of prelates was not regarded as an abuse but was justified by a widely held doctrine of royal theocracy, which had been formulated by the churchmen themselves during the troubles of the ninth and tenth centuries, when stronger kings seemed the only possible alternative to sheer anarchy. The coronation ritual of England compared the Anglo-Saxon king to Moses, Joshua, David, and Solomon. The emperors of the Ottonian and Salian dynasties were acclaimed as vicars of God on earth. Eleventh-century kings did not merely designate bishops but actually conferred ecclesiastical office upon the men of their choice by "investing" them with ring and staff, the symbols of episcopal power. The reformers came to challenge this practice of lay investiture: in doing so, they challenged the whole basis of royal authority.

It was almost inevitable that the challenge would be made. The reformers, who were interested in returning to the discipline of the early church, devoted much energy to making collections of ancient canons to serve as a guide for their own programs. They found plenty of texts (genuine and forged) to uphold the supreme power of the pope in the church but few to support the claims of the kings. According to early church law, a bishop was supposed to be canonically elected and then consecrated to his office by fellow bishops. The prevailing practice of lay investiture had no canonical basis, as Cardinal Humbert pointed out in a treatise written about 1055. "How does it pertain to lay persons," he wrote, "to distribute ecclesiastical sacraments and episcopal grace, that is to say, the crozier staffs and rings with which episcopal consecration is principally effected?" The objection to lay investiture was not, however, merely a matter of canonical theory. There could be no permanent, effective reform movement directed from Rome if appointments to all major ecclesiastical offices, including the papacy itself, were to be made at the whim of secular kings who might or might not be reasonably responsible Christian rulers. Henry III had made scrupulously good appointments. His predecessor, Conrad II, had made notoriously bad ones. No one knew what line Henry IV might take when he became old enough to govern his kingdom.

For the reformers, the most important thing of all was that they should retain control of the papal office. Accordingly, in 1059, during the short pontificate of Nicholas II (1059–1061), a council at Rome promulgated a decree regulating the conduct of papal elections. It excluded both the lay Roman aristocratic factions and the imperial government from effective participation in the choice of future popes and entrusted papal elections to the cardinals of the Roman church. This system, with various procedural modifications, has existed ever since. In case such a bold innovation should meet with violent resistance, Nicholas II made an alliance at this point with the Norman warriors who had been settling in southern Italy during the preceding half century.

The same council that promulgated the papal election decree also declared vaguely that in future no priest should receive any church from a layman, but there was no attempt to enforce this decree or to spell out its precise meaning. The decree concerning the papacy, on the other hand, was put into effect as soon as the next vacancy arose in 1061. . . .

On the other hand, Hildebrand, who became pope in 1073 as Gregory VII, was a passionate reformer, convinced that he was God's chosen instrument to purify the church, and also convinced that enduring reform could be carried out only if royal control over ecclesiastical appointments was broken once and for all. Hildebrand seems to have been utterly heedless of the political implications of this demand. He was God's vicar, so he thought. If a king dared to resist his divine mission, so much the worse for the king. The most obvious criticism that has been made of Hildebrand is that, not content with the spiritual authority of a priest, he tried to make himself temporal overlord of Europe as well. But this seems an oversimplification. He did not value the authority of temporal rulers so highly as to want it for himself; rather, he despised worldly power and refused to recognize in it any intrinsic dignity or real right to consideration. Kings and feudal princes were to him essentially police chiefs who had the duty of using coercive force to achieve objectives laid down by the church. When Hildebrand was accused by contemporaries of seeking to usurp royal power, he seems to have been genuinely puzzled and indignant at the charge. He did not covet the policeman's office. He regarded it as beneath his dignity.

In February 1075 Gregory VII promulgated the decree against lay investiture that led to the struggle with Henry IV of Germany. (The text of the original decree has been lost. The text that follows is from a reenactment of 1078.)

Decree Against Lay Investiture

INASMUCH AS WE HAVE LEARNED that, contrary to the establishments of the holy fathers, the investiture with churches is, in many places, performed by lay persons; and that from this cause many disturbances arise in the church by which the Christian religion is trodden under foot: we decree that no one of the clergy shall receive the investiture with a bishopric or abbey or church from the hand of an emperor or king or of any lay person, male or female. But if he shall presume to do so he shall clearly know that such investiture is bereft of apostolic authority, and that he himself shall lie under excommunication until fitting satisfaction shall have been rendered.

In March 1075 the propositions that follow, the so-called Dictatus Papae, were set down in the pope's official register. They are thought to be chapter headings for a proposed collection of canons.

Dictatus Papae

1. That the Roman Church was founded by God alone.
2. That the Roman Pontiff alone is rightly to be called universal.
3. That he alone can depose or reinstate bishops.
4. That his legate, even if of lower grade, takes precedence, in a council, of all bishops and may render a sentence of deposition against them.
5. That the Pope may depose the absent.
6. That, among other things, we also ought not to stay in the same house with those excommunicated by him.
7. That for him alone it is lawful to enact new laws according to the needs of the time, to assemble together new congregations, to make an abbey of a canonry; and, on the other hand, to divide a rich bishopric and unite the poor ones.
8. That he alone may use the imperial insignia.
9. That the Pope is the only one whose feet are to be kissed by all princes.
10. That his name alone is to be recited in churches.

11. That his title is unique in the world.
12. That he may depose Emperors.
13. That he may transfer bishops, if necessary, from one See to another.
14. That he has power to ordain a cleric of any church he may wish.
15. That he who has been ordained by him may rule over another church, but not be under the command of others; and that such a one may not receive a higher grade from any bishop.
16. That no synod may be called a general one without his order.
17. That no chapter or book may be regarded as canonical without his authority.
18. That no sentence of his may be retracted by any one; and that he, alone of all, can retract it.
19. That he himself may be judged by no one.
20. That no one shall dare to condemn a person who appeals to the Apostolic See.
21. That to this See the more important cases of every church should be submitted.
22. That the Roman Church has never erred, nor ever, by the witness of Scripture, shall err to all eternity.
23. That the Roman Pontiff, if canonically ordained, is undoubtedly sanctified by the merits of St. Peter; of this St. Ennodius, Bishop of Pavia, is witness, many Holy Fathers are agreeable and it is contained in the decrees of Pope Symmachus the Saint.
24. That, by his order and with his permission, subordinate persons may bring accusations.
25. That without convening a synod he can depose and reinstate bishops.
26. That he should not be considered as Catholic who is not in conformity with the Roman Church.
27. That the Pope may absolve subjects of unjust men from their fealty.

By the end of 1075 it had become clear that Henry IV would not obey the pope's decree against lay investiture. In December Gregory wrote to the king rebuking him and threatening excommunication. Henry then summoned a synod of German bishops and, having won their support, denounced Gregory as a usurper.

Henry IV's Letter to Gregory VII, 1076

HENRY, KING NOT BY usurpation, but by the pious ordination of God, to Hildebrand, now not Pope, but false monk:

You have deserved such a salutation as this because of the confusion you have wrought; for you left untouched no order of the

Church which you could make a sharer of confusion instead of honor, of malediction instead of benediction.

For to discuss a few outstanding points among many: Not only have you dared to touch the rectors of the holy Church—the archbishops, the bishops, and the priests, anointed of the Lord as they are—but you have trodden them under foot like slaves who know not what their lord may do. In crushing them you have gained for yourself acclaim from the mouth of the rabble. You have judged that all these know nothing, while you alone know everything. In any case, you have sedulously used this knowledge not for edification, but for destruction, so greatly that we may believe Saint Gregory, whose name you have arrogated to yourself, rightly made this prophesy of you when he said: "From the abundance of his subjects, the mind of the prelate is often exalted, and he thinks that he has more knowledge than anyone else, since he sees that he has more power than anyone else."

And we, indeed, bore with all these abuses, since we were eager to preserve the honor of the Apostolic See. But you construed our humility as fear, and so you were emboldened to rise up even against the royal power itself, granted to us by God. You dared to threaten to take the kingship away from us—as though we had received the kingship from you, as though kingship and empire were in your hand and not in the hand of God.

Our Lord, Jesus Christ, has called us to kingship, but has not called you to the priesthood. For you have risen by these steps: namely, by cunning, which the monastic profession abhors, to money; by money to favor; by favor to the sword. By the sword you have come to the throne of peace, and from the throne of peace you have destroyed the peace. You have armed subjects against their prelates; you who have not been called by God have taught that our bishops who have been called by God are to be spurned; you have usurped for laymen the bishops' ministry over priests, with the result that these laymen depose and condemn the very men whom the laymen themselves received as teachers from the hand of God, through the imposition of the hands of bishops. [*Gregory had instructed the laity not to receive sacraments from priests who refused to obey his reform decrees directed against concubinage, simony, and other abuses—Ed.*]

You have also touched me, one who, though unworthy, has been anointed to kingship among the anointed. This wrong you have done to me, although as the tradition of the holy Fathers has taught, I am to be judged by God alone and am not to be deposed for any crime unless—may it never happen—I should deviate from the Faith. For the prudence of the holy bishops entrusted the judgment and the deposition even of Julian the Apostate not to themselves, but to God alone. The true pope Saint Peter also exclaims, "Fear God, honor the king." You, however, since you do not fear God, dishonor me, ordained of Him.

Wherefore, when Saint Paul gave no quarter to an angel from heaven if the angel should preach heterodoxy, he did not except you who are now teaching heterodoxy throughout the earth. For he says, "If anyone, either I or an angel from heaven, preach any other gospel unto you than that which we have preached unto you, let him be accursed." Descend, therefore, condemned by this anathema and by the common judgment of all our bishops and of ourself. Relinquish the Apostolic See which you have arrogated. Let another mount the throne of Saint Peter, another who will not cloak violence with religion but who will teach the pure doctrine of Saint Peter.

I, Henry, King by the grace of God, together with all our bishops, say to you: Descend! Descend!

Gregory replied by declaring Henry excommunicated and deposed from his kingship.

Deposition of Henry IV, 1076

O BLESSED PETER, prince of the Apostles, mercifully incline thine ear, we [*sic*] pray, and hear me, thy servant, whom thou hast cherished from infancy and hast delivered until now from the hand of the wicked who have hated and still hate me for my loyalty to thee. Thou art my witness as are also my Lady, the Mother of God, and the blessed Paul, thy brother among all the saints, that thy Holy Roman Church forced me against my will to be its ruler. I had no thought of ascending thy throne as a robber, nay, rather would I have chosen to end my life as a pilgrim than to seize upon thy place for earthly glory and by devices of this world. Therefore, by thy favor, not by any works of mine, I believe that it is and has been thy will, that the Christian people especially committed to thee should render obedience to me, thy especially constituted representative. To me is given by thy grace the power of binding and loosing in Heaven and upon earth.

Wherefore, relying upon this commission, and for the honor and defense of thy Church, in the name of Almighty God, Father, Son and Holy Spirit, through thy power and authority, I deprive King Henry, son of the emperor Henry, who has rebelled against thy Church with unheard-of audacity, of the government over the whole kingdom of Germany and Italy, and I release all Christian men from the allegiance which they have sworn or may swear to him, and I forbid anyone to serve him as king. For it is fitting that he who seeks to diminish the glory of thy Church should lose the glory which he seems to have.

And, since he has refused to obey as a Christian should or to return to the God whom he has abandoned by taking part with excommunicated persons, has spurned my warnings which I gave him for his soul's welfare, as thou knowest, and has separated himself from thy Church and tried to rend it asunder, I bind him in the bonds of anathema in thy stead and I bind him thus as commissioned by thee, that the nations may know and be convinced that thou art Peter and that upon thy rock the son of the living God has built his Church and the gates of hell shall not prevail against it.

The pope's condemnation of Henry touched off a rebellion in Germany. Henry was defeated and undertook to appear before a Diet of German princes at Augsburg in February 1077. The pope was to preside over the Diet, and the future of the German kingship was to be decided there. To avoid the humiliation of a public trial before his subjects, Henry journeyed over the Alps in December 1076, met the pope at Canossa, and pleaded as a penitent sinner to be released from the papal sentence of excommunication. Gregory subsequently wrote the following account of the episode to the German princes.

Gregory VII's Letter to the German Princes

WHEREAS, FOR LOVE OF JUSTICE you have made common cause with us and taken the same risks in the warfare of Christian service, we have taken special care to send you this accurate account of the king's penitential humiliation, his absolution and the course of the whole affair from his entrance into Italy to the present time.

According to the arrangement made with the legates sent to us by you we came to Lombardy about twenty days before the date at which some of your leaders were to meet us at the pass and waited for their arrival to enable us to cross over into that region. But when the time had elapsed and we were told that on account of the troublous times—as indeed we well believe—no escort could be sent to us, having no other way of coming to you we were in no little anxiety as to what was our best course to take.

Meanwhile we received certain information that the king was on the way to us. Before he entered Italy he sent us word that he would make satisfaction to God and St. Peter and offered to amend his way of life and to continue obedient to us, provided only that he should obtain from us absolution and the apostolic blessing. For a long time we delayed our reply and held long consultations, reproaching him bitterly through messengers back and forth for his outrageous conduct, until finally, of his own accord and without any show of hostility or defiance, he came with a few followers to the fortress of Canossa where we were staying. There, on three successive days, standing before the castle gate, laying aside all royal insignia, barefooted and in coarse attire, he ceased not with many tears to beseech the apostolic help and comfort until all who were present or who had heard the story were so moved by pity and compassion that they pleaded his cause with prayers and tears. All marveled at our unwonted severity, and some even cried out that we were showing, not the seriousness of apostolic authority, but rather the cruelty of a savage tyrant.

At last, overcome by his persistent show of penitence and the urgency of all present, we released him from the bonds of anathema and received him into the grace of Holy Mother Church, accepting from him the guarantees described below, confirmed by the signatures of the abbot of Cluny, of our daughters, the Countess Matilda and the Countess Adelaide, and other princes, bishops and laymen who seemed to be of service to us.

And now that these matters have been arranged, we desire to come over into your country at the first opportunity, that with God's help we may more fully establish all matters pertaining to the peace of the Church and the good order of the land. For we wish you clearly to understand that, as you may see in the written guarantees, the whole negotiation is held in suspense, so that our coming and your unanimous consent are in the highest degree necessary. Strive, therefore, all of you, as you love justice, to hold in good faith the obligations into which you have entered. Remember that we have not bound ourselves to the king in any way except by frank statement—as our custom is—that he may expect our aid for his safety and his honor, whether through justice or through mercy, and without peril to his soul or to our own.

Once Henry had made his peace with the pope, he found new support in Germany. Many of the princes thought that Gregory had betrayed them by dealing with Henry individually before the proposed Diet had met. The dissident princes elected an anti-king, Rudolf, and civil war broke out once more. After hesitating for three years, Gregory agreed to support Rudolf and condemned Henry for a second time in March 1080.

Second Deposition of Henry IV, 1080

O BLESSED PETER, chief of the Apostles, and thou, Paul, teacher of the Gentiles, deign, I pray, to incline your ears to me and mercifully to hear my prayer. Ye who are disciples and lovers of the truth, aid me to tell the truth to you, freed from all falsehood so hateful to you, that my brethren may be more united with me and may know and understand that through faith in you, next to God and his mother Mary, ever virgin, I resist the wicked and give aid to those who are loyal to you. . . .

The kings of the earth, and the princes, both secular and clerical, have risen up, courtiers and commons have taken counsel together against the Lord, and against you, his anointed, saying, "Let us burst their chains and throw off their yoke," and they have striven utterly to overwhelm me with death or banishment.

Among these especially Henry, whom they call "king," son of

the emperor Henry, has raised his heel against your Church in conspiracy with many bishops, as well ultramontanes as Italians, striving to bring it under his control by overturning me. Your authority withstood his insolence and your power defeated it. In confusion and humiliation he came to me in Lombardy begging for release from his excommunication. And when I had witnessed his humiliation and after he had given many promises to reform his way of life, I restored him to communion only, but did not reinstate him in the royal power from which I had deposed him in a Roman synod. Nor did I order that the allegiance of all who had taken oath to him or should do so in future, from which I had released them all at that same synod, should be renewed. I held this subject in reserve in order that I might do justice as between him and the ultramontane bishops and princes, who in obedience to your Church had stood out against him, and that I might establish peace amongst them, as Henry himself had promised me to do on his oath and by the word of two bishops.

. . . But the aforesaid Henry together with his supporters, not fearing the perils of disobedience—which is the crime of idolatry— incurred excommunication by preventing a conference and bound himself [again] in the bonds of anathema and caused a great multitude of Christians to be delivered to death, churches to be scattered abroad and almost the whole kingdom of the Germans to be desolated.

Wherefore, trusting in the justice and mercy of God and of his most worshipful mother Mary, ever virgin, and relying upon your authority, I place the aforesaid Henry, whom they call "king," and all his supporters under excommunication and bind them with the chains of anathema. And again forbidding him in the name of Almighty God and of yourselves to govern in Germany and Italy, I take from him all royal power and state. I forbid all Christians to obey him as king, and I release all who have made or shall make oath to him as king from the obligation of their oath. May Henry and his supporters never, so long as they may live, be able to win victory in any encounter of arms. But that Rudolf, whom the Germans have chosen for their king in loyalty to you, may rule and protect the kingdom of the Germans, I grant and allow in your name. And relying upon your assurance, I grant also to all his faithful adherents absolution of all their sins and your blessing in this life and the life to come. For as Henry is justly cast down from the royal dignity for his insolence, his disobedience and his deceit, so Rudolf, for his humility, his obedience and his truthfulness is granted the power and the dignity of kingship.

And now, most holy fathers and princes, I pray you to take such action that the whole world may know and understand that if you are able to bind and loose in Heaven, you are able also on earth to grant and to take away from everyone according to his deserts empires, kingdoms, principalities, dukedoms, marquisates, earldoms and the property of all men. You have often taken patriarchates, primacies, archbishoprics and bishoprics away from wicked and unworthy men and have granted them to pious holders. And if you can give judgment in spiritual things, what may we not believe as to your power over secular things? Or, if you can judge the angels who guide all haughty princes, what can you [not] do to their servants? Now let kings and all princes of the earth learn how great is your power, and let them fear to neglect the commands of your Church. And against the aforesaid Henry send forth your judgment so swiftly that all men may know that he falls and is overwhelmed, not by chance but by your power— and would that it were to repentance, that his soul be saved in the day of the Lord!

————————————————

We are fortunate in having a detailed explanation of Gregory's ideas and intentions written by the pope himself in a letter to Bishop Hermann of Metz (March 1081). The excerpts that follow give the main points of Gregory's argument.

Gregory VII's Letter to Hermann of Metz, 1081

You ASK US TO FORTIFY YOU against the madness of those who babble with accursed tongues about the authority of the Holy Apostolic See not being able to excommunicate King Henry as one who despises the law of Christ, a destroyer of churches and of the empire, a promoter and partner of heresies, nor to release anyone from his oath of fidelity to him; but it has not seemed necessary to reply to this request, seeing that so many and such convincing proofs are to be found in Holy Scripture. Nor do we believe that those who abuse and contradict the truth to their utter damnation do this as much from ignorance as from wretched and desperate folly. And no wonder! It is ever the way of the wicked to protect their own iniquities by calling upon others like themselves; for they think it of no account to incur the penalty of falsehood.

To cite but a few out of the multitude of proofs: Who does not remember the words of our Lord and Savior Jesus Christ: "Thou art Peter and on this rock I will build my Church, and the gates of hell shall not prevail against it. And I will give thee the keys of the kingdom of heaven and whatsoever thou shalt bind on earth shall be bound in heaven and whatsoever thou shalt loose on earth shall be loosed in heaven." Are kings excepted here? Or are they not of the sheep which the Son of God committed to St. Peter? Who, I ask, thinks himself excluded from this universal grant of the power of binding and loosing to St. Peter unless, perchance, that unhappy man who, being unwilling to bear the yoke of the Lord, subjects himself to the burden of the Devil and refuses to be numbered in the flock of Christ? His wretched liberty shall profit him nothing; for if he shakes off from his proud neck the power divinely granted to Peter, so much the heavier shall it be for him in the day of judgment.

. . . To whom, then, the power of opening and closing Heaven is given, shall he not be able to judge the earth? God forbid! Do you remember what the most blessed Apostle Paul says: "Know ye not that we shall judge angels? How much more things that pertain to this life?"

*   *   *

But now, to return to our point: Is not a sovereignty invented by men of this world who were ignorant of God subject to that which the providence of Almighty God established for his own glory and graciously bestowed upon the world? The Son of God we believe to be God and man, sitting at the right hand of the Father as High Priest, head of all priests and ever making intercession for us. He despised the kingdom of this world wherein the sons of this world puff themselves up and offered himself as a sacrifice upon the cross.

Who does not know that kings and princes derive their origin from men ignorant of God who raised themselves above their fellows by pride, plunder, treachery, murder—in short, by every kind of crime—at the instigation of the Devil, the prince of this world, men blind with greed and intolerable in their audacity? If, then, they strive to bend the priests of God to their will, to whom may they more properly be compared than to him who is chief over all the sons of pride? For he, tempting our High Priest, head of all priests, son of the Most High, offering him all the kingdoms of this world, said: "All these will I give thee if thou wilt fall down and worship me."

Does anyone doubt that the priests of Christ are to be considered as fathers and masters of kings and princes and of all believers? Would it not be regarded as pitiable madness if a son should try to rule his father or a pupil his master and to bind with unjust obligations the one through whom he expects to be bound or loosed, not only on earth but also in heaven? Evidently recognizing this the emperor Constantine the Great, lord over all kings and princes throughout almost the entire earth, as St. Gregory relates in his letter to the emperor Mauritius, at the holy synod of Nicaea took his place below all the bishops and did not venture to pass any judgment upon them but, even addressing them as gods, felt that they ought not to be subject to his judgment but that he ought to be bound by their decisions.

Pope Gelasius, urging upon the emperor Anastasius not to feel himself wronged by the truth that was called to his attention said: "There are two powers, O august Emperor, by which the world is governed, the sacred authority of the priesthood and the power of kings. Of these the priestly is by so much the greater as they will have to answer for kings themselves in the day of divine judgment;" and a little further: 'Know that you are subject to their judgment, not that they are to be subjected to your will."

In reliance upon such declarations and such authorities, many prelates have excommunicated kings or emperors. If you ask for illustrations: Pope Innocent excommunicated the emperor Arcadius because he consented to the expulsion of St. John Chrysostom from his office. Another Roman pontiff deposed a king of the Franks, not so much on account of his evil deeds as because he was not equal to so great an office, and set in his place Pippin, father of the emperor

Charles the Great, releasing all the Franks from the oath of fealty which they had sworn to him. And this is often done by Holy Church when it absolves fighting men from their oaths to bishops who have been deposed by apostolic authority. So St. Ambrose, a holy man but not bishop of the whole Church, excommunicated the emperor Theodosius the Great for a fault which did not seem to other prelates so very grave and excluded him from the Church. He also shows in his writings that the priestly office is as much superior to royal power as gold is more precious than lead. He says: "The honor and dignity of bishops admit of no comparison. If you liken them to the splendor of kings and the diadem of princes, these are as lead compared to the glitter of gold. You see the necks of kings and princes bowed to the knees of priests, and by the kissing of hands they believed that they share the benefit of their prayers." And again: "Know that we have said all this in order to show that there is nothing in this world more excellent than a priest or more lofty than a bishop."

Your Fraternity should remember also that greater power is granted to an exorcist when he is made a spiritual emperor for the casting out of devils, than can be conferred upon any layman for the purpose of earthly dominion.* All kings and princes of this earth who live not piously and in their deeds show not a becoming fear of God are ruled by demons and are sunk in miserable slavery. Such men desire to rule, not guided by the love of God, as priests are, for the glory of God and the profit of human souls, but to display their intolerable pride and to satisfy the lusts of their mind. Of these St. Augustine says in the first book of his Christian doctrine: "He who tries to rule over men—who are by nature equal to him—acts with intolerable pride." Now if exorcists have power over demons, as we have said, how much more over those who are subject to demons and are limbs of demons! And if exorcists are superior to these, how much more are priests superior to them!

Furthermore, every Christian king when he approaches his end asks the aid of a priest as a miserable suppliant that he may escape the prison of hell, may pass from darkness into light and may appear at the judgment seat of God freed from the bonds of sin. But who, laymen or priest, in his last moments has ever asked the help of any earthly king for the safety of his soul? And what king or emperor has power through his office to snatch any Christian from the might of the Devil by the sacred rite of baptism, to confirm him among the sons of God and to fortify him by the holy chrism? Or—and this is the greatest thing in the Christian religion—who among them is able by his own word to create the body and blood of the Lord? or to whom among them is given the power to bind and loose in Heaven and upon earth? From this it is apparent how greatly superior in power is the priestly dignity.

Or who of them is able to ordain any clergyman in the Holy Church—much less to depose him for any fault? For bishops, while

---

* The office of exorcist was the lowest in the ecclesiastical hierarchy, ranking below bishops, priests, and deacons—Ed.

they may ordain other bishops, may in no wise depose them except by authority of the Apostolic See. How, then, can even the most slightly informed person doubt that priests are higher than kings? But if kings are to be judged by priests for their sins, by whom can they more properly be judged than by the Roman pontiff?

The issue of lay investiture was never settled in the lifetimes of Gregory VII and Henry IV. Pope Calixtus II and King Henry V reached a compromise agreement, known as the "Concordat of Worms," in 1122. The king gave up the actual ceremony of "investiture" with ring and staff but retained considerable influence in the nomination of bishops. Some historians regard this outcome as a victory for Gregorian principles. Others point out that the king "gave up the shadow but retained the substance" of royal power.

Concordat of Worms, 1122

PRIVILEGE OF THE EMPEROR

IN THE NAME OF Holy and Indivisible Trinity. I, Henry, by the grace of God August Emperor of the Romans, for the love of God and of the Holy Roman Church and of the lord Pope Calixtus and for the healing of my soul, do surrender to God, to the Holy Apostles of God, Peter and Paul, and to the Holy Roman Church all investiture through ring and staff; and do agree that in all churches throughout my kingdom and empire there shall be canonical elections and free consecration. I restore to the same Roman Church all the possessions and temporalities ["regalia"] which have been abstracted until the present day either in the lifetime of my father or in my own and which I hold; and I will faithfully aid in the restoration of those which I do not hold. . . .

PRIVILEGE OF THE POPE

I, Bishop Calixtus, servant of the servants of God, concede to you, beloved son Henry—by the grace of God August Emperor of the Romans—that the election of those bishops and abbots in the German kingdom who belong to the kingdom shall take place in your presence without simony and without any violence; so that if any discord occurs between the parties concerned, you may—with the counsel or judgment of the metropolitan and the co-provincials—give your assent and assistance to the party which appears to have the better case. The candidate elected may receive the "regalia" from you through the sceptre and he shall perform his lawful duties to you for them. . . .

3 Modern Views on Gregory VII

Philip Hughes presented Gregory VII as a zealous church reformer with no political ambitions.

FROM *A History of the Church* BY *Philip Hughes*

THE PRINCIPLE THAT GIVES UNITY to the whole of Gregory VII's varied activity is his ever present realisation that he is responsible to God for all the souls entrusted to him. Political activity may be a necessary means, but the end in view is always wholly supernatural. The pope must answer to God for the souls of kings no less than for those of priests and peasants; for kings too must keep God's law, or find themselves in hell for all eternity. And to William the Conqueror Gregory VII wrote this explicitly, "If then, on that day of terrible judgment it is I who must represent you before the just judge whom no lies deceive and who is the creator of all creatures, your wisdom will itself understand how I must most attentively watch over your salvation, and how you, in turn, because of your salvation and that you may come to the land of the living, must and ought to obey me without delay." There is nothing new in this: it is but a particular application of the general principle that the shepherd is charged to guide the whole flock which Gelasius I, for example, had stated no less explicitly to the emperor Anastasius six hundred years before St. Gregory VII. Nor, despite the ingenuity of later, anti-papal, historians—was this meant as a thinly-disguised means of bringing about a political system in which the pope should rule all the affairs of the Christian world. Nowhere in the pope's own declarations is there any hint that he hoped for such a position, nor in the multitudinous writings of his supporters, whether publicists or canonists, that argue for the rights he did claim; nor is there any sign that the emperor believed this to be Gregory's aim, or any of the emperor's men. To none of the pope's contemporaries, to none of those who were at the heart of the struggle, did it ever occur, even to allege, that what Gregory VII was aiming at was to be the emperor of a Christian world state.

Henry IV, too, had his problems, and chief among them that of recovering what the crown had lost during his own long minority. Appointments to sees, and the accompanying simony, were at the moment important political expedients. This return to the evil ways of his grandfather had already, in the last years of Alexander II, led to difficulties between Henry and the Holy See; and the candidate to whom the king had sold the see of Constance was, thanks to the pope, denied consecration. Despite the king, a council, presided over by papal legates, was held at Mainz (1071) and the bishop-elect of Constance was compelled to resign. In another dispute, which divided the bishops and abbots of Thuringia—where the allocation of tithes was in question—the king had intervened to prevent an appeal to Rome. It was already more than evident that, in Henry IV, the reform movement faced the most serious opponent who had so far arisen. In Germany itself his determination to dominate the great feudatories could only end in war, and in 1073 a general revolt broke out which came near to sweeping him away altogether. In his despair Henry appealed to the pope, acknowledging his simony and his many usurpations in the matter of ecclesiastical jurisdiction, asking for aid and humbly promising amendment of his life. Gregory VII had already planned his policy with regard to the German king. He was not by nature an intransigent. He would do his best, by kindly warnings, to turn Henry from an opponent into an ally of the reform. Only when he proved obdurate did the pope return to the drastic remedies of Cardinal Humbert and Nicholas II in order to secure the freedom of religion. Already, in September, 1073, he had forbidden the new Bishop of Lucca to receive investiture from the king, and now came the king's submission and appeal. . . .

This decree of February, 1075, against lay investiture was not intended, the thing seems certain, as an aggressive move against the princes—still less was it an act which especially envisaged Henry IV; the pope was in no hurry to promulgate the decree to princes generally, and his policy in applying the law varied greatly. In the English kingdom of William the Conqueror, for example, where simony had no place in the royal appointments, and where king and bishops were at one with the pope in the work of reform, Gregory VII never raised the question at all. The new law was, indeed, "a preventive weapon designed to assist the struggle against simony." In a country where simony on the part of the king was systematic, and the king hardened in his resolve to maintain the system, conflict—speedy conflict—was inevitable; and such was the case with Henry IV. And, as the decree was a challenge to Henry IV so too were the blunt declarations of the *Dictatus Papae* a challenge to the feudalised ecclesiastical princes who occupied the sees of Germany. In these twenty-seven terse propositions king and bishops were warned that the pope's laws against simony, clerical ill-living, and the usurpation of rights to appoint were no dead letter, and that none, whatever his rank, would escape the sanctions enacted against those who broke these laws.

Geoffrey Barraclough argued that Gregory was primarily interested in "breaking the power of the crown. . . ."

FROM *Origins of Modern Germany* BY *Geoffrey Barraclough*

BEHIND ALL THE RESOUNDING APPEALS to principle, therefore, we must take into account the play and cross-currents of political interests. The opponents of Henry were a motley crowd, pursuing divergent interests; and it required all the efforts of the pope and his legates to hold them together. Gregory was not fastidious in his choice of allies. Unlike the earlier reforming popes, from Leo IX to his own immediate predecessor, Alexander II, he was not by birth a member of the episcopal aristocracy, and this was probably one reason why he did not hesitate to enlist the people and stir up popular discontent both in Germany and Italy. His alliance with the Pataria and the nascent communes in Lombardy brought him into disrepute; but he showed no hesitation in allying with forces which were seeking to revolutionize the existing order for secular ends. He appeared to throw over principle in favour of expediency when, in order to find a safe refuge at the moment of Henry IV's triumph, he came to terms with the Norman prince, Robert Guiscard, who had been excommunicated for occupying papal territory. His alliance with the German aristocracy was hard to justify save on political grounds; for its leaders were notorious despoilers of the Church, and the civil war unleashed by the excommunication of Henry in 1076 resulted in unparalleled depredation, of which Gregory himself was well aware as early as 1078. By his alliance with the German aristocracy Gregory sacrificed the prospect of lasting reform; for reform, in the eyes of the German princes, was little more than a pretext—as once again in the sixteenth century it was to be a pretext—to enable them to establish control over the Church. It is difficult to escape the conclusion that, for Gregory and his successors, the end justified the means, and that they were more intent on breaking the power of the crown within the Church than on purifying the Church from abuse. In this the Gregorian party was at loggerheads with the moderate party within the Church, the party led by Peter Damiani, which held that the movement against lay investiture was a false step which fatally distracted attention from the main task, the moral regeneration of the Church, and that cooperation with the monarchy was not impossible. For the Gregorians, on the other hand, the political struggle with the German monarchy overshadowed all else; and in this struggle they were willing to ally indiscriminately with princes, Saxons, Normans, communes and Pataria. In this sense the Gregorian movement was a truly revolutionary movement; just as its ultimate object was to overturn the accepted order, so its instruments and methods and alliances and associations were revolutionary in character. For the attack on the Salian monarchy and its principles of government, the papacy mobilized every revolutionary force within the empire: hence the unparalleled fury when the cataclysm was, at last, let loose.

Gerd Tellenbach saw Gregory as the leader of a religious revolution.

FROM *Church, State and Christian Society* BY *Gerd Tellenbach*

THE AGE OF THE Investiture Controversy may rightly be regarded as the culmination of medieval history; it was a turning point, a time both of completion and of beginning. It was the fulfillment of the early Middle Ages, because in it the blending of the Western European peoples with Christian spirituality reached a decisive stage. On the other hand, the later Middle Ages grew directly out of the events and thoughts of the decades immediately before and after the year 1100; as early as this the general lines, the characteristic religious, spiritual, and political views of later times had been laid down, and the chief impulses for subsequent development given.

The great struggle had a threefold theme. On the basis of a deeper understanding of the nature of the Catholic Church, an attempt was made to remodel three things: first, the relations of clergy and laity with each other; secondly, the internal constitution of the church, through the imposition of papal primacy; and thirdly, the relations of church and world. The first of these disputed questions in which lay investiture played the most important part has given its name to the whole period. The old state-controlled constitution of the church and the proprietary church system, both of them factors of the first importance in the conversion of the Western European peoples and in the building up of church organization, had originated in pre-Christian times and were at bottom foreign to the church's real nature. Only after long and wearisome struggles did the church succeed in restricting them or incorporating them in the structure of the canon law. Lay investiture and the whole proprietary system were, however, burning questions only for a few centuries during the earlier part of the Middle Ages; but the battle between episcopalism and papalism has, in spite of periodic interruptions, intermittently disturbed the church from the earliest Christian era down to the present time, and the relationship between Christianity and the secular state is, for Catholics and Protestants alike, still a deeply moving and not yet completely solved question. The best-known and most violent conflict to which it ever gave rise, the struggle in which church and state met each other in the pride of their strength and fully armed with their natural weapons, was the Investiture Controversy.

It will never be quite possible to discover what were the real causes of the great 11th-century crisis in Christian history; many factors in the political life of the times which did in fact coalesce to form a developing situation the main lines of which are clear, might, it seems to us now, have operated very differently. It is just as difficult to explain why it was that men who were capable of great things came together in Rome at that particular time, and above all, why at the critical moment the demonic figure of the greatest of the popes occupied the throne of the Prince of the Apostles. Only a very wide-ranging view can make clear, even in part the concurrence of events out of which the new age was born, for only thus will due influence be assigned to the advanced stage which the christianization of the world had then reached. Ecclesiastical organization had spread far and wide, monastic religion had taken a strong hold on men and made them more concerned for their souls' health, had spurred them on to greater conscientiousness and made them more anxious for the purity and right order of the church. Thus a new and victorious strength was lent to the old belief in the saving grace of the sacraments and to the hierarchical conceptions based on their administration. Out of this arose the conviction that the Christian peoples of the West formed the true City of God, and as a result the leaders of the church were able to abandon their ancient aversion from the wickedness of worldly men and to feel themselves called upon to reorder earthly life in accordance with divine precept. In the 11th century the position had not yet been reached where the pope, the imperial Lord of the Church, appointed and confirmed the kings of the earth and watched over and judged their actions, but the enormous advance made by Gregory VII had opened the way for this, and he himself had already realized more of it in practice than any single one of his successors was able to do. Gregory stands at the greatest—from the spiritual point of view perhaps the only—turning point in the history of Catholic Christendom; in his time the policy of converting the world gained once and for all the upper hand over the policy of withdrawing from it: the world was drawn into the church, and the leading spirits of the new age made it their aim to establish the "right order" in this united Christian world. In their eyes, however, the most immediate task seemed to be that of successfully asserting the supremacy of the "Servant of the servants of God" over the kings of the earth.

Gregory VII was not particularly notable for his faithfulness to tradition. He was at heart a revolutionary; reform in the ordinary sense of the word, which implies little more than the modification and improvement of existing forms, could not really satisfy him. He desired a drastic change and could be content with nothing short of the effective realization on earth of justice, of the "right order," and of "that which ought to be." "The Lord hath not said 'I am Tradition,' " he once wrote, "but 'I am the Truth.' " And yet, in spite of this reaction against the merely traditional, Gregory himself embodied the essence of Catholic tradition in a peculiarly characteristic manner; this fact shows, therefore, how instinctive and unreasoning—in a sense, how primitive—his faith was. Catholicism was to him the directive principle of life itself. For him the age-old Catholic ideas of righteousness (*justitia*), a Christian hierarchy (*ordo*), and a proper standing for everyone before God and man (*libertas*) were the core of religious experience, and their realization the purpose of life here on earth. It would be incorrect to treat these and related ideas as the personal discoveries of St. Augustine or any other particular individual among the early Fathers, or to attempt to trace out exactly the stages by which Gregory is supposed to have inherited them; they are in reality an inseparable part of the Catholic faith and can only be understood on that assumption. It is just as wide of the mark to suggest that ideas such as these were discovered for the first time by Gregory and his contemporaries, or that they were in any significant way remolded during the Gregorian period; Gregory's real service was to leaven the earthly lump with the principles of Catholicism and to make the latter, in a manner hitherto undreamed of, a really decisive force in politics. His aim was to bring the Kingdom of God on earth, as he saw it in his mind, nearer to realization, and to serve the cause of order, justice, and "freedom." "He was indeed," writes Bernold of St. Blasien, "a most zealous propagator (*institutor*) of the Catholic religion and a most determined defender of the freedom of the Church. For he did not wish the clergy to be subject to the power of the laity, but desired them to excel all laymen by their holiness and by the dignity of their order."

*   *   *

The enormous strength of the ecclesiastical claim to world domination is only to be explained if we recognize how profoundly religious were its roots; it grew directly out of the fundamental tenets of the Catholic faith, and failure to realize this is the reason why many earlier attempts at explanation must be rejected as mistaken or insufficient. To derive a demand for worldwide power from asceticism and the flight from the earthly life, as some historians have done, is to ascribe an improbable religious perversity to the church; and there is equally little logic in the connected theory that the church wished to reduce the world to subjection in order to be free from it. Nor is it possible to suppose that the emperor was deprived of the right of investiture simply in order that the clergy alone should represent the unity of the church. Further, it is scarcely a half-truth to assert, as is sometimes done, that Gregory VII combated lay influence in order to increase his opportunities of carrying out moral reform and the internal reorganization of the church. This was only part of his purpose; as we have seen, the real reason for the action he took lies deeper: his moral principles were outraged by the mere fact that the laity were occupying a position which, according to the sacramental conception of the hierarchy, was not really theirs at all. A true understanding of the ideas of Gregory VII and of post-Gregorian Catholicism about the relation of the spiritual power to the world, and of the origins of these ideas themselves, can only be reached by going right back to the belief in the incarnation of God in Christ. This is the most fundamental of the church's beliefs, for in the church the saving grace of the incarnation has become an ever-present reality, and all the church's institutions find in this belief their *raison d'être* and their ultimate justification. Mystical and hierarchical trains of thought arise naturally from the belief that God comes down from heaven to man, and that the multitude of His priests serves as the steps by which He descends. If, therefore, the church and the hierarchy of its servants have a part in the mediating office of Christ, if they exist in order to link heaven and earth, then it is only just that the world should meekly accept their guidance and be subject to them. This demand forms a principle the validity of which Catholicism is always bound to assert; it is this principle which must ultimately decide its attitude toward the state, although in recent centuries it has been applied less in the purely political field than during the Middle Ages, and more as a claim to the care of souls and to moral leadership.

4 *The Program of Innocent III*

Innocent's sermons preached at his own consecration and on its anniversary contained some of his highest claims for the papacy.

FROM *Sermons on the Consecration of a Pontiff*

WHO AM I OR WHAT is my father's house that I should sit higher than kings and hold a throne of glory? For to me it is said in the person of the prophet, "I have set thee over nations and over kingdoms, to root up and to pull down, and to waste and to destroy, and to build and to plant" (Jeremias 1:10). To me also is said in the person of the apostle, "I will give to thee the keys of the kingdom of heaven. And whatsoever thou shalt bind upon earth it shall be bound in heaven, etc." (Matthew 16:19) . . . thus the others were called to a part of the care but Peter alone assumed the plenitude of power. You see then who is this servant set over the household, truly the vicar of Jesus Christ, successor of Peter, anointed of the lord, a God of Pharoah, set between God and man, lower than God but higher than man, who judges all and is judged by no one. . . .

*   *   *

This bride (the Roman church) has not come to me empty-handed, but has brought me a dowry rich beyond price, a plenitude of spiritual powers and a broad extent of temporal powers. For others were called to a part of the care but Peter alone assumed the plenitude of power. As a sign of spiritual power she (the church) has conferred on me a mitre, as a sign of temporal power she has given me a crown, the mitre for priesthood, the crown for kingship.[1]

In 1202 Count William of Montpellier requested the pope to legitimize his two bastard sons. Innocent refused, saying that the matter lay within the jurisdiction of the king of France. But he took advantage of the occasion to expound at length his views on the powers of the papacy.

---

[1] The pope was temporal ruler of the Papal States in Italy. It may be that Innocent referred only to this "kingship."

The Decretal, Per Venerabilem

YOUR HUMILITY HAS REQUESTED through our venerable brother the archbishop of Arles, who came to the apostolic see, that we deign to adorn your sons with the title of legitimacy so that defect of birth would not hinder their succeeding to you. That the apostolic see has full power in the matter seems clear from the fact that, having examined various cases, it has given dispensations to some illegitimate sons —not only natural sons but also those born of adultery—legitimizing them for spiritual functions so that they could be promoted to be bishops. From this it is held to be more likely and reputed to be more credible that it is able to legitimize children for secular functions, especially if they acknowledge no superior among men who has the power of legitimizing except the Roman pontiffs; for greater care and authority and worthiness are required in spiritual affairs and so it seems that what is conceded in greater matters is lawful also in lesser ones. . . .

Now the king [of France] acknowledges no superior in temporal affairs and so, without injuring the right of anyone else, he could submit himself to our jurisdiction and did so. It seemed to some indeed that he could perhaps have granted the dispensation himself, not as a father to his sons but as a prince to his subjects. But you know that you are subject to others so you cannot submit yourself to us in this matter without injuring them unless they give consent, and you are not of such authority that you have the power of granting a dispensation yourself.

Motivated therefore by these considerations we granted to the king the favor requested, deducing from both the Old and the New Testaments that, not only in the patrimony of the church where we wield full power in temporal affairs, but also in other regions, we may exercise temporal jurisdiction incidentally after having examined certain cases. It is not that we want to prejudice the rights of anyone else or to usurp any power that is not ours, for we are not unaware that Christ answered in the Gospel "Render to Caesar the things that are Caesar's, and to God the things that are God's" (Luke 20:25). Consequently, when he was asked to divide an inheritance between two men, he said, "Who hath appointed me judge over you?" (Luke 12:14). But in Deuteronomy this is contained, "If thou perceive that there be among you a hard and doubtful matter in judgement between blood and blood, cause and cause, leprosy and leprosy: and thou see that the words of the judges within thy gates do vary: arise and go up to the place the lord thy God shall choose. And thou shalt come to the priests of the Levitical race, and to the judge that shall be at that time: and thou shalt ask of them, and they shall shew thee the truth of the judgement. And thou shalt do whatsoever they shall say that preside in the place which the Lord shall choose, and what they shall teach thee according to his law; and thou shalt follow their sentence: neither shalt thou decline to the right hand nor to the left hand. But he that will be proud, and refuse to obey the commandment of the priest who ministereth at that time to the Lord, thy God, and the decree of the judge, that man shall die, and thou shalt take away the evil from Israel." (Deuteronomy 17:8–12). Now since the word "Deuteronomy" means a second law, it is proved from the meaning of the word itself that what is laid down there is to be observed also in the New Testament. For the place which the Lord has chosen is known to be the apostolic see from this, that the Lord founded it on himself as its corner stone, for, when Peter was fleeing from the city, the Lord, wanting him to return to the place that he had chosen and being asked by him, "Lord whither goest thou?" replied, "I am going to Rome to be crucified again." Peter understood that this was meant for him and at once returned to the place.

The priests of the Levitical race are our brothers who, according to Levitical law, act as our coadjutors in the discharge of the priestly office. There is indeed a priest or judge above them to whom the Lord said in the person of Peter, "Whatsoever thou shalt bind upon earth it shall be bound also in heaven" (Matthew 16:19). This is the vicar of him who is a priest for ever according to the order of Melchisedech, established by God as judge of the living and the death. Three kinds of judgement are distinguished, the first between blood' and blood by which civil crimes are signified, the last between leper and leper by which ecclesiastical crimes are signified, and a middle kind, between cause and cause, which refers to both civil and ecclesiastical cases. In these matters, whenever anything difficult or ambiguous has arisen, recourse is to be had to the apostolic see, and if anyone disdains to obey its sentence out of pride he shall be condemned to death to "take away the evil from Israel," that is to say he shall be separated from the communion of the faithful, as if dead, by a sentence of excommunication. Paul too, writing to the Corinthians to explain the plenitude of power, said, "Know you not that we shall judge angels? How much more the things of this world?" (1 Corinthians 6:3.) Accordingly [the apostolic see] is accustomed to exercise the office of secular power sometimes and in some things by itself, sometimes and in some things through others.

Therefore, although we decided to grant a dispensation to the sons of the aforesaid king of the French . . . we do not assent to your petition although we embrace your person with arms of especial affection and are willing to show you special favor in any matters in which we can do so honorably and in accordance with God's will.

In 1202 the German princes complained that Innocent was seeking to control the imperial election, a matter that, they said, belonged solely to the prince electors. Innocent responded with a carefully reasoned explanation of his claim to have a decisive voice in the election.

The Decretal, Venerabilem

AMONG OTHER THINGS CERTAIN princes urge this objection particularly, that our venerable brother the bishop of Palestrina, legate of the apostolic see, acted as either an elector [of the emperor] or as a judge of the election. If as an elector, he put his sickle in a stranger's harvest and, by intervening in the election, detracted from the dignity of the princes; if as a judge, he seems to have proceeded incorrectly since one of the parties was absent and should not have been judged contumacious when he had not been cited to appear. We indeed by virtue of our office of apostolic service, owe justice to each man and, just as we do not want our justice to be usurped by others, so too we do not want to claim for ourselves the rights of the princes. We do indeed acknowledge, as we should, that the princes, to whom this belongs by right and ancient custom, have the right and power to elect a king who is afterwards to be promoted emperor; and especially so since this right and power came to them from the apostolic see which transferred the Roman empire from the Greeks to the Germans in the person of the great Charles. But the princes should acknowledge, and indeed they do acknowledge, that right and authority to examine the person elected as king, who is to be promoted to the imperial dignity, belong to us who anoint, consecrate and crown him; for it is regularly and generally observed that the examination of a person pertains to the one to whom the laying-on of hands belongs. If the princes elected as king a sacrilegious man or an excommunicate, a tyrant, a fool or a heretic, and that not just by a divided vote but unanimously, ought we to anoint, consecrate and crown such a man? Of course not. Therefore, replying to the objection of the princes, we maintain that our legate the bishop of Palestrina, our dearly beloved brother in Christ, did not act as either an elector . . . or as a judge when he approved King Otto and rejected Duke Philip. And so he in no way usurped the right of the princes or acted against it. Rather he exercised the office of one who declared that the king was personally worthy and the duke personally unworthy to obtain the imperial dignity, not considering so much the zeal of the electors as the merits of those elected. . . .

It is clear from law and precedent that, if the votes of the princes are divided in an election, we can favor one of the parties after due warning and a reasonable delay, especially after the unction, consecration and coronation are demanded of us, for it has often happened that both parties demanded them. For if the princes after due warning and delay cannot or will not agree, shall the apostolic see then lack an advocate and defender and be penalized for their fault? . . .

In 1204 Innocent tried to settle a feudal dispute between the kings of France and England. The French bishops complained that he was exceeding the bounds of his

authority in judging a purely secular case. Again Innocent
replied with a carefully reasoned statement of his right to
intervene.

The Decretal, Novit

LET NO ONE SUPPOSE that we wish to diminish or disturb the jurisdiction and power of the king when he ought not to impede or restrict our jurisdiction and power. Since we are insufficient to exercise all our own jurisdiction why should we want to usurp another's? But the Lord says in the Gospel, "If thy brother shall offend against thee, go, and rebuke him between thee and him alone. If he shall hear thee thou shalt gain thy brother. And if he will not hear thee, take with thee one or two more, that in the mouth of two or three witnesses every word may stand. And if he will not hear them, tell the church. And if he will not hear the church let him be to thee as the heathen and the publican" (Matthew 18:15); and the king of England is ready, so he asserts, to prove fully that the king of the French is offending against him and that he has proceeded according to the evangelical rule in rebuking him and, having achieved nothing, is at last telling it to the church. How then can we, who have been called to the rule of the universal church by divine providence, obey the divine command if we do not proceed as it lays down, unless perhaps [King Philip] shows sufficient reason to the contrary before us or our legate. For we do not intend to judge concerning a fief, judgement on which belongs to him—except when some special privilege or contrary custom detracts from the common law—but to decide concerning a sin, of which the judgement undoubtedly belongs to us, and we can and should exercise it against any-one. . . .

The emperor Theodosius decreed and Charles, ancestor of the present king, confirmed that "If anyone has a legal case . . . and chooses to take it before the bishop of the most holy see, without question and even if the other party objects, he is to be sent to the bishop's court with the statements of the litigants." This, however, we pass over in humility for we do not rely on human statutes but on divine law since our power is not from man but from God.

No man of sound mind is unaware that it pertains to our office to rebuke any Christian for any mortal sin and to coerce him with ecclesiastical penalties if he spurns our correction. That we can and should rebuke is evident from the pages of both the Old and New Testaments. . . . That we can and should coerce is evident from what the Lord said to the prophet who was among the priests of Anathoth, "Lo I have set thee over nations and over kingdoms to root up and to pull down and to waste, and to destroy, and to build, and to plant" (Jeremias 1:10). No one doubts that all mortal sin must be rooted up and destroyed and pulled down. Moreover, when the Lord gave the keys of the kingdom of heaven to blessed Peter, he said, "Whatsoever thou shalt bind upon earth, it shall be bound also in heaven: and whatsoever thou shalt loose on earth it shall be loosed also in heaven" (Matthew 16:19). . . . But it may be said that kings are to be treated differently from others. We, however, know that it is written in the divine law, "You shall judge the great as well as the little and there shall be no difference of persons" (*cf*. Deuteronomy 1:17). . . . Although we are empowered to proceed in this fashion against any criminal sin in order to recall the sinner from error to truth and from vice to virtue, this is especially so when it is a sin against peace, peace which is the bond of love. . . . Finally, when a treaty of peace was made between the kings and confirmed on both sides by oaths which, however, were not kept for the agreed period, can we not take cognizance of such a sworn oath, which certainly belongs to the judgement of the church, in order to re-establish the broken treaty of peace? . . .

Some historians have seen in Innocent's writing a claim to temporal lordship over the whole world. They maintain that "his goal was papal world dominion."

FROM *Kirchengeschichte Deutschlands* BY *Albert Hauck*

HE KNEW HOW TO WIN influence in all things. But in this thousand-fold splintered occupation he never lost sight of the goal: the enforcement of papal rule in the Church and in the world.

He had not established the goal, but found it when he entered office. The ideology of the curia had known a long development. He had taken it over and restated it in the old formulas; even the proofs he used, the comparisons with which he illustrated it, were borrowed. But the borrowings sounded different, as the emphasis was put on this or that point. Here is a case in point. With Nicholas I, the statement of the supreme hegemony of the papacy arose out of the necessity to safeguard moral and religious interests; with Gregory VII, conviction of duty to accomplish Church reform provided the starting point. With Innocent, these points of reference were put aside; his goal was papal world dominion. Now was the pope no more primarily priest, but before all a secular lord. The language is concerned with his rule over Church and world, so before "Church" a "not only" should be introduced: not only the Church but also the world has been given to him to rule; so the latter appears in opposition to the former as the greater concern. Therefore, to Innocent, the essence of papal power was in the union of the priestly and the imperial dignity. In conformity with its origins and purpose, the imperial power belonged to the pope. Italy stood at the pinnacle of the world because Rome, as a result of its primacy, was the seat of priesthood and of kingship. It was logical for Innocent to take up the theory of the translation of the emperorship from the Greeks to the Romans by the popes. Now it won a more sure acceptance for the first time. It is still more remarkable that he stated the relationship of the two powers from the viewpoint of feudal law: the pope invested the candidate with the imperial power. It followed therefore that the pope had the right to examine the imperial election and to decide whether or not the candidate was fit for imperial office; and, again, the assertion that the pope should be empowered to raise an illegal candidate to the throne if he recognized him as the more suitable person was only one result. He treated princes in general as he did the emperors. That he allowed both to remain was a concession to actuality, not to any conviction that the secular power was necessary. His ideal was much more the immediate hegemony of the papacy in the world. Only if the secular and spiritual power were united in the hand of the pope could a situation completely satisfactory to the Church be established. Especially was this the natural situation for Italy.

We cannot deny that the assertion of an all-powerful papacy was at this point revolutionary. What was natural was exalted over historical right. Innocent had the courage to draw the conclusions of his viewpoint. Especially did his theory of the binding-force of oaths prove this point. It was not enough that he conferred on the pope the right to repeal every oath according to his free judgment; he asserted that oaths sworn by princes generally were opposed to God and his precepts, *i.e.*, the papal commands, and were not binding. For it would not be permitted to him to hold the truth who would not hold God as the Truth. Therewith the permanence of all constitutional provisions of the secular power was left to the will and judgment of one man. The highest bishop of the Church was the absolute ruler in secular affairs. But, at the same time, the transformation of the papacy to a primarily secular power was accomplished.

> R. W. and A. J. Carlyle analyzed the letters of Innocent III given previously and concluded that they did not assert a claim to unlimited temporal power.

FROM *A History of Mediaeval Political Theory in the West* BY R. W. and A. J. Carlyle

THE STATEMENTS WHICH we have now to examine are with one exception contained in Decretal letters of Pope Innocent III; and we will do well to remember that there were few of the great Popes of the Middle Ages who set the ecclesiastical power higher, and who actually exercised a greater influence in Europe.

*   *   *

. . . Innocent avoids here all suggestion that the spiritual power is supreme over the secular within the sphere of the latter.

We find that this position of Innocent is maintained consistently in other important Decretals which deal with the matter. There is a very remarkable illustration of this in a Decretal dealing with the dispute as to the election of Philip of Suabia and Otto to the empire. Innocent III had interfered in this case to annul the election of Philip and to confirm the election of Otto. At first sight it would seem as though this were obviously an assertion by the Pope of his authority over the secular power, and of a claim to take the appointment into his own hands and to supersede the electors. But Innocent is at great pains to disclaim this construction of his action. Some of the princes had complained that the Papal legate had taken upon himself the office of an elector or "cognitor," and maintained that this was wholly illegitimate. Innocent denies that he had done this, and says that his legate had only acted as a "*denunciator*,"—that is, he had declared Philip to be unworthy and Otto to be worthy to receive the empire. Innocent recognises that the electors have the right and authority to elect the king, who is afterwards to be promoted to the empire; they have the right by law and ancient custom, and the Pope must specially recognise this, as it was the Apostolic See which transferred the empire from the Greeks to the Germans. But, on the other hand, Innocent urges that the princes must recognise that the right and authority of examining the person elected belongs to the Pope, who is to anoint and consecrate and crown him, for it is a general principle that the examination of a person belongs to him who is to lay hands on him, and the princes cannot maintain that if they elected, even unanimously, a sacrilegious or excommunicated person, the Pope would be obliged to consecrate and crown him. Finally, he claims that if the electors are divided, he has the right to decide in favour of one of the parties, and urges that this was done in the case of the disputed election of Lothair and Conrad.

It is interesting to observe how carefully Innocent guards his own action, and disclaims the intention of overriding the legitimate rights of the electors. His claim, in fact, no doubt amounts to an enormous invasion of the rights of the electors of the empire—that is, his claim to determine which of the candidates should be acknowledged in case of a disputed election; but, as we have pointed out, there were important precedents for his claiming a great and even a paramount share in determining the election. His refusal to acknowledge an excommunicated person was only a natural extension of the principle that excommunication involved deposition. It is very significant that he makes no claim to any abstract political supremacy over the empire; his silence is indeed very significant, for, as we have seen, there was at least one phrase in the canonical collection of Gratian which seemed to imply that the successors of Peter had received this authority from Christ Himself.

This conclusion is confirmed by the terms of another important Decretal letter of Innocent, written to the French bishops, defending his claim to arbitrate between the French and English kings. He begins by repudiating the notion that he desires to disturb or diminish the jurisdiction or authority of the French king, while he expects that the French king, on his part, will not interfere with the Papal jurisdiction and authority. The Lord in the Gospels had bidden an injured person appeal to the Church, and the king of England asserted that the king of the French had transgressed against him, and that he therefore had appealed to the Church, and the Pope, therefore, could not refuse to hear him. He disclaims all desire to judge as to the question of the fief, and he recognises that any question of this kind belongs to the feudal lord—that is, in this case, to the king of the French, unless, indeed, the *jus commune* had been altered by a special *privilegium* or by custom; but he claims the right to decide as to the "sin," for it cannot be doubted that jurisdiction on this point belongs to the Pope. The French king should not consider it derogatory to his dignity to submit in this matter to the Apostolic judgment; and he appeals to the words of the Emperor Valentinian and to a decree of the Emperor Theodosius, which, as he says, had been renewed by the Emperor Charles, under which any party to a suit might, even without the consent of the other party, appeal to the bishop. No sane person, he continues, can doubt that it is the duty of the Pope to rebuke men for mortal sin, and if they refuse to submit, to subject them to ecclesiastical censure: it cannot be pretended that kings are exempt from this jurisdiction. If this is true of all sins, how much more must it be true with regard to a transgression against peace, and he appeals to the warning of the Gospel directed against those who refuse to receive the messenger of peace. . . .

The claim which Innocent makes is no doubt one of great magnitude, but it is very necessary that we should observe carefully the grounds upon which Innocent rests it, and notice again the omission of all claim to act as one who possessed a political authority superior to that of the temporal sovereign. His claim is based on two principles —first, the religious one, that any question of transgression or sin by one man against another belonged to the Church's jurisdiction, and therefore especially any transgression against peace, and any question concerning the obligation or violation of oaths; secondly, on the appeal to a legal ordinance, which permitted any party in a civil suit at any time to take the case from the civil court to that of the bishop. . . .

Whatever may be said as to the grounds upon which Innocent bases his claims, it is quite clear that we have here no pretension to a general political supremacy. . . .

5 The Final Struggle—
Frederick II and Innocent IV

*Frederick II's complex personality was described by the
contemporary Franciscan chronicler Salimbene.. The ver-
sion that follows is from a translation and paraphrase of
Salimbene's work by G. G. Coulton.*

Frederick II: A Contemporary View

To SALIMBENE, AS TO DANTE, Frederick was a man of heroic propor-
tions in his very sins. "Of faith in God he had none; he was crafty,
wily, avaricious, lustful, malicious, wrathful; and yet a gallant man at
times, when he would show his kindness or courtesy; full of solace,
jocund, delightful, fertile in devices. He knew to read, write, and
sing, and to make songs and music. He was a comely man, and well-
formed, but of middle stature. I have seen him, and once I loved him,
for on my behalf he wrote to Bro. Elias, Minister-General of the Friars
Minor, to send me back to my father. Moreover, he knew to speak
with many and varied tongues, and, to be brief, if he had been rightly
Catholic, and had loved God and His Church, he would have had few
emperors his equals in the world." [Salimbene] goes on to enumerate
several specimens of the Emperor's "curiosities" or "excesses," though
for sheer weariness he will not tell them all. Frederick cut off a notary's
thumb who had spelt his name *Fredericus* instead of *Fridericus*. Like
Psammetichus in Herodotus, he made linguistic experiments on the
vile bodies of hapless infants, "bidding foster-mothers and nurses to
suckle and bathe and wash the children, but in no wise to prattle or
speak with them; for he would have learnt whether they would speak
the Hebrew language (which had been the first), or Greek, or Latin,
or Arabic, or perchance the tongue of their parents of whom they had
been born. But he laboured in vain, for the children could not live
without clappings of the hands, and gestures, and gladness of counte-
nance, and blandishments." Again, "when he saw the Holy Land,
(which God had so oft-times commended as a land flowing with milk
and honey and most excellent above all lands,) it pleased him not, and
he said that if the God of the Jews had seen *his* lands of Terra di
Lavoro, Calabria, Sicily, and Apulia, then He would not so have commended the land which He promised to the Jews." Again, he compelled "Nicholas the Fish," whom his mother's curse had condemned
to an amphibious life, to dive and fetch his golden cup a second time
from the very bottom of Charybdis: in which repeated attempt the
poor man knew that he must perish. Fifthly, "he enclosed a living man
in a cask that he might die there, wishing thereby to show that the

soul perished utterly, as if he might say the word of Isaiah 'Let us eat and drink, for to-morrow we die.' For he was an Epicurean; wherefore, partly of himself and partly through his wise men, he sought out all that he could find in Holy Scripture which might make for the proof that there was no other life after death, as for instance 'Thou shalt destroy them, and not build them up': and again 'Their sepulchres shall be their houses for ever.' Sixthly, he fed two men most excellently at dinner, one of whom he sent forthwith to sleep, and the other to hunt; and that same evening he caused them to be disembowelled in his presence, wishing to know which had digested the better: and it was judged by the physicians in favour of him who had slept. Seventhly and lastly, being one day in his palace, he asked of Michael Scot the astrologer how far he was from the sky, and Michael having answered as it seemed to him, the Emperor took him to other parts of his kingdom as if for a journey of pleasure, and kept him there several months, bidding meanwhile his architects and carpenters secretly to lower the whole of his palace hall. Many days afterwards, standing in that same palace with Michael, he asked of him, as if by the way, whether he were indeed so far from the sky as he had before said. Whereupon he made his calculations, and made answer that certainly either the sky had been raised or the earth lowered; and then the Emperor knew that he spake truth." Yet Salimbene is careful to note that Frederick's cruelties might justly be excused by the multitude of his open and secret enemies, and that he had a saving sense of humour. "He was wont at times to make mocking harangues before his court in his own palace, speaking for example after the fashion of the Cremonese ambassadors," at whose tediousness and outward flourishes our good friar laughs again later on. "Moreover, he would suffer patiently the scoffings and mockings and revilings of jesters, and often feign that he heard not. For one day, after the destruction of Victoria by the men of Parma, he smote his hand on the hump of a certain jester, saying 'My Lord Dallio, when shall this box be opened?' To whom the other answered, ' 'Tis odds if it be ever opened now, for I lost the key in Victoria.' The Emperor, hearing how this jester recalled his own sorrow and shame, groaned and said, with the Psalmist, 'I was troubled, and I spoke not.' If any had spoken such a jest against Ezzelino da Romano, he would without doubt have let him be blinded or hanged. . . ."

The following sentence of deposition was enacted by Innocent IV at the general council of Lyons (June 1245).

Deposition of the Emperor, 1245

HE HAS COMMITTED four very grave offences, which can not be covered up by any subterfuge (we say nothing for the moment about his other crimes); he has abjured God on many occasions; he has wantonly broken the peace which had been re-established between the Church and the Empire; he has also committed sacrilege by causing to be imprisoned the Cardinals of the holy Roman Church and the prelates and clerics, regular and secular, of other churches, coming to the Council which our predecessor had summoned; he is also accused of heresy not by doubtful and flimsy but by formidable and clear proofs. . . .

We therefore, who are the vicar, though unworthy, of Jesus Christ on earth and to whom it was said in the person of blessed Peter the Apostle; "Whatsoever thou shalt bind on earth," etc., show and declare on account of the above-mentioned shameful crimes and of many others, having held careful consultation with our brethren and the holy Council, that the aforesaid prince—who has rendered himself so unworthy of all the honour and dignity of the Empire and the kingdom and who, because of his wickedness, has been rejected by God from acting as king or Emperor—is bound by his sins and cast out and deprived of all honour and dignity by God, to which we add our sentence of deprivation also. We absolve for ever all who owe him allegiance in virtue of an oath of fealty from any oath of this kind; and we strictly forbid by Apostolic authority that any one should obey him or look upon him henceforth as king or Emperor, and we decree that whoever shall in the future afford him advice, help or goodwill as if he were Emperor or king, shall fall "ipso facto" under the binding force of excommunication. But let those in the same Empire whose duty it is to look to the election of an Emperor, elect a successor freely. We shall make it our business to provide for the aforesaid kingdom of Sicily as seems best to us with the advice of our brethren.

In response to the papal sentence Frederick denounced Pope Innocent IV and the whole existing state of the church. He addressed this protest generally to "the kings of Christendom."

Frederick's Reply

WHAT IS IMPLIED by our maltreatment is made plain by the presumption of Pope Innocent IV for, having summoned a council—a general council he calls it—he has dared to pronounce a sentence of deposition against us who were neither summoned nor proved guilty of any deceit or wickedness, which sentence he could not enact without grievous prejudice to all kings. You and all kings of particular regions have everything to fear from the effrontery of such a prince of priests when he sets out to depose us who have been divinely honored by the imperial diadem and solemnly elected by the princes with the approval of the whole church at a time when faith and religion were flourishing

among the clergy, us who also govern in splendor other noble kingdoms; and this when it is no concern of his to inflict any punishment
on us for temporal injuries even if the cases were proved according to
law. In truth we are not the first nor shall we be the last that this
abuse of priestly power harasses and strives to cast down from the
heights; but this indeed you also do when you obey these men who
feign holiness, whose ambition hopes that "the whole Jordan will
flow into their mouth" (*cf.* Job 40:18). O if your simple credulity
would care to turn itself "from the leaven of the Scribes and Pharisees
which is hypocrisy" (Luke 12:1) according to the words of the
Savior, how many foul deeds of that court you would be able to
execrate, which honor and shame forbid us to relate. The copious
revenues with which they are enriched by the impoverishment of many
kingdoms, as you yourself know, make them rage like madmen. Christians and pilgrims beg in your land so that Patarene heretics may eat
in ours. You are closing up your houses there to build the towns of
your enemies here. These poor followers of Christ are supported and
enriched by your tithes and alms, but by what compensating benefit,
or what expression of gratitude even do they show themselves beholden
to you? The more generously you stretch out a hand to these needy
ones the more greedily they snatch not only the hand but the arm,
trapping you in their snare like a little bird that is the more firmly
entangled the more it struggles to escape.

We have concerned ourselves to write these things to you for the
present, though not adequately expressing our intentions. We have
decided to omit other matters and to convey them to you more secretly;
namely the purpose for which the lavishness of these greedy men
expends the riches of the poor; what we have found out concerning
the election of an emperor if peace is not established at least superfi-
cially between us and the church, which peace we intend to establish
through eminent mediators; what dispositions we intend to make
concerning all the kingdoms in general and each in particular; what
has been arranged concerning the islands of the ocean; how that court
is plotting against all princes with words and deeds which could not
be concealed from us who have friends and subjects there, although
clandestinely; with what stratagems and armies trained for war we
hope in this coming spring to oppress all those who now oppress us,
even though the whole world should set itself against us.

But whatever our faithful subjects, the bearers of this letter,
relate to you you may believe with certainty and hold as firmly as if
St. Peter had sworn to it. Do not suppose on account of what we ask
of you that the magnanimity of our majesty has been in any way
bowed down by the sentence of deposition launched against us, for
we have a clean conscience and so God is with us. We call him to
witness that it was always our intention to persuade the clergy of
every degree that they should continue to the end as they were in the
early days of the church living an apostolic life and imitating the
Lord's humility, and that it was our intention especially to reduce
those of highest rank to this condition. Those clergy [of former days]
used to see angels and were resplendent with miracles; they used to

heal the sick, raise the dead and subject kings and princes to themselves by holiness, not by arms. But these, drunk with the pleasures of the world and devoted to them, set aside God, and all true religion is choked by their surfeit of riches and power. Hence, to deprive such men of the baneful wealth that burdens them to their own damnation is a work of charity. You and all princes, united with us, ought to be as diligent as you can in achieving this end so that, laying aside all superfluities and content with modest possessions, they may serve the God whom all things serve.

The following letter was composed on behalf of Innocent IV and circulated as a reply to Frederick's protest. It provides a final statement of the pope's claims over the empire.

A Defense of the Deposition

WHEN A SICK MAN who cannot be helped by mild remedies undergoes a surgical incision or cautery, he rages in bitterness of spirit against his doctor and, unable to endure the harsh remedies of the cure, complains that he is being cruelly murdered by the one who is performing a health giving operation. In the same way a condemned man is sometimes inflamed against his condemner . . . and mistakenly blames what he suffers, not on his own faults, but on the injustice of the judge. . . . If then Frederick, formerly emperor, strives to accuse with noisy widespread complaints the sacred judge of the universal church through whom he was declared cast down by God so that he might no longer rule or reign, it ought not to seem anything new or marvellous, for he is behaving in the same fashion as others in like case. . . .

He says to be sure that the order of justice was perverted and that he was not legitimately cited or convicted but was criminally condemned by a judge who had no power to judge him. Thus in his usual fashion he persists in reducing to nothing the primacy of apostolic dignity which Peter, the head of all the faithful, and his successors are known to have received not from man but from God, as all agree. Indeed anyone who claims to be exempt from the authority of his vicar diminishes the authority of God and does not acknowledge God, the son of God, to be inheritor and lord of all things. For we act as a general legate on earth of the king of kings who bestowed on the prince of the apostles, and in him on us, a plenitude of power to bind and loose not only everyone but everything "whatsoever," including all things in the more general neuter form lest any thing or any business should seem to be exempted. Also the teacher of the gentiles showed this plenitude to be unbounded when he said "Do you not know that we shall judge angels? How much more the things of this world" (1

Corinthians 6:3). Did he not explain that the power given over angels extended also to temporalities in order to make it understood that lesser things also are subordinated to those to whom greater ones are subject?

The eternal priesthood of Christ established under his grace in the unshakeable see of Peter is to be credited not with less power but with much more than the ancient priesthood that served for a time according to the forms of the law, and yet God said to the priesthood of those times, "See I have set thee over nations and over kingdoms to root up and to pull down, and to waste and to destroy, and to build and to plant" (Jeremias 1:10); not only "over nations" but also "over kingdoms," so that it might be known that power was committed over both. We read that many pontiffs of the Old Testament used this power, removing from the royal throne by the authority divinely committed to them not a few kings who had become unworthy to rule. It remains then that the Roman pontiff can exercise his pontifical judgment at least incidentally over any Christian of any condition whatsoever especially if no one else can or will render to him the justice that is due, and particularly by reason of sin. Thus he may decree that any sinner whose contumacy has brought him to the depths of depravity is to be held as "a publican and a stranger" and outside the body of the faithful so that, by implication at least, he is deprived of the power of any temporal rulership that he had, for such power most certainly cannot be borne outside the church, since there, where everything builds for Hell, there is no power ordained by God. Therefore they do not discern shrewdly or know how to investigate the origins of things who think that the apostolic see first received rule over the empire from the prince Constantine, for this rule is known to have been inherent in the apostolic see naturally and potentially beforehand. For our Lord Jesus Christ, the son of God, was a true king and true priest after the order of Melchisedech just as he was true man and true God, which he made manifest by now using the honor of royal majesty before men, now exercising on their behalf the dignity of the pontificate before the Father, and he established not only a pontifical but a royal monarchy in the apostolic see, committing to Peter and his successors control over both an earthly and a heavenly empire, which was adequately signified in the plurality of the keys, so that the vicar of Christ might be known to have received the power of judging over the heavens in spiritual things through the one key that we have received, over the earth in temporal things through the other.

In truth when Constantine was joined to the Catholic church through the faith of Christ he humbly resigned to the church the inordinate tyranny that he had formerly exercised outside it—and we, respectfully imitating the fathers of old, retain the insignia of the princely dress left by him as a permanent symbol and full pledge of the mystical reason for this resignation—and he received within the church from Christ's vicar, the successor of Peter, a duly ordered power of sacred rulership which thenceforward he used legitimately for the punishment of the evil and the praise of the good, and he who had formerly abused a power permitted to him afterwards exercised an authority bestowed on him. For both swords of either administration are kept in the flock of the faithful church as the assertion of the apostle shows and the divine authority agrees, whence anyone who is not within it has neither sword. Moreover neither is to be regarded as outside Peter's sphere of right, since the Lord did not say concerning the material sword "Lay it aside," but, "Return your sword to its sheath" (Matthew 26:52) meaning that you shall not yourself exercise it in future. He said expressly "your sword" and "your sheath" to indicate that there resided with his vicar, the head of the church militant, not the actual exercise of this sword, which was forbidden to him by divine command, but rather the authority by which this same exercise is made manifest in the service of the law for the punishment of the wicked and the defence of the good. For indeed the power of this material sword is implicit in the church but it is made explicit through the emperor who receives it from the church, and this power which is merely potential when enclosed in the bosom of the church becomes actual when it is transferred to the prince. This is evidently shown by the ceremony in which the supreme pontiff presents to the emperor whom he crowns a sword enclosed in a sheath. Having taken it the emperor draws the sword and by brandishing it indicates that he has received the exercise of it. It was from this sheath, namely from the plenitude of the apostolic power, that the aforesaid Frederick received the sword of his exalted principate, and in order that he might defend the peace of the church, not disturb it. . . .

For Philip Hughes, Innocent IV was above all a brave defender of the liberties of the church in a time of great danger.

FROM *A History of the Church* BY *Philip Hughes*

[IN RESPONSE TO THE request of Innocent IV] for a conference, the emperor replied by sending to him his two chief advisers, the legists Piero della Vigna and Thaddeus of Suessa.

The negotiations ended with Frederick renewing all his old pledges to restore the papal territory he occupied, and granting an amnesty to all who had recently fought against him, even the Lombards being included. This was on Holy Thursday, 1244, but before April was out the pope had to protest that Frederick was once again breaking his sworn word. Frederick, in reply, suggested a personal conference between himself and Innocent. The pope, with the memory of the last two years fresh in his mind,* was, however, too wary to be caught. This time he would retain his freedom and use it to attack. Disguised as a knight he fled to Genoa, and thence crossed the Alps to Lyons, a city where the sovereign was the archbishop and his chapter

---

* [*The papacy was vacant from 1241 to 1243—Ed.*]

—nominally within the emperor's jurisdiction, but close to the protective strength of the King of France, St. Louis IX.

The council which Gregory IX had planned, Innocent realised. It met at Lyons in the July of 1245, two hundred bishops and abbots attending. This first General Council of Lyons is unique in that its main purpose was a trial. The emperor was making it his life's aim to restore the ancient subordination of religion to the State. The pope was determined to destroy him, to end for all time this power which had once, for so long, enslaved the Church and which, for a good century now, had never ceased its attack on the Church's restored independence. There was to be no return to the bad days which had preceded St. Leo IX and St. Gregory VII. Since none but a fool would place any reliance on Frederick's oaths, Frederick should be deposed.

On July 7, 1245, the council, in solemn public session, listened to the recital of the emperor's crimes and shifty, insincere repentances. Then, despite the pleading of Thaddeus of Suessa, it accepted the decree of deposition.

Frederick, in reply, circularised the reigning princes of Europe. If the decree of deposition is perhaps the clearest expression yet of the theory of the papal power over temporal rulers as such, Frederick's riposte may be read as the first manifesto of the "liberal" state. For it sets out, against the papal practice, a complete, anti-ecclesiastical theory. All the anti-sacerdotal spirit of the heresies of the previous century find here new, and more powerful, expression. The supremacy of the *sacerdotium* is denounced as a usurpation, and anti-clericalism, applied now for the first time to the pagan conception of the omnipotent state—a doctrine popularised through the rebirth of Roman Law—offers itself as a world force with the destruction of the *sacerdotium* as its aim. Thanks to the imperial legists, and especially to the genius of the two already mentioned, the new point of view is set forth imperishably in this manifesto, and the princes of Christendom are invited to join with the emperor in his attempt to destroy the common enemy. The Church, they are told, is part of the State, and, for all that Frederick guards against any overt denial of the pope's authority, the Catholic prince is, for him, inevitably a kind of Khalif. It is this prince's mission to keep religion true to itself, to reform it whenever necessary, and to bring it back to the primitive simplicity of the gospel. Frederick had indeed revealed himself. The theory is the most subversive of heresies, and it is the emperor, the pledged defender of orthodoxy, the prince the very *raison d'être* of whose office is orthodoxy's defence, who is its inventor and patron. His reply to the excommunication more than justified the attitude of Gregory IX, and Innocent's initiative.

*   *   *

Historians—Catholics equally with the rest—have not spared bitter words for Innocent IV. His inflexibility and determination in the long struggle, and the rigidity they developed, are set side by side with the more seductive and picturesque traits of his treacherous enemy. The treachery is forgotten, and the menace too, which the family tradition presented, in pity for the tragic end of the dynasty. But Innocent IV was one of the greatest of the popes none the less, a man whom nothing short of the high ideals of St. Gregory VII inspired. His tragic pontificate knew few peaceful days; his greatest achievement, like all violent victories, left a mixed legacy to his successors. But again, the achievement was great; and it sets him at least as high as the predecessor and namesake who, in popular fancy, has altogether overshadowed him. One of the writers best qualified to judge Innocent IV, the scholar who edited his registers, sums it up thus: "The Holy See had survived one of the most terrible crises it had ever faced, thanks to the *sang-froid*, the decision and the incomparable tenacity of this great pope."

―――――――――

> *A. L. Smith presented a less favorable account of Innocent IV.*

FROM *Church and State in the Middle Ages* BY *A. L. Smith*

'THE STARS SHALL FALL from heaven, the rivers turn to blood, sooner than the Pope abandon his purpose.' This was the word that went forth from Lyons. The purpose was war to the death in Germany. Let us see what were the weapons. The first was the German episcopate. Under Barbarossa they had been state officials. Innocent III had transformed them into an independent hierarchy. Gregory IX tried intimidation, but Innocent IV appealed to mundane motives, local associations, individual interests. No Church principle, no Church property was allowed to stand in the way of securing one of these new proselytes. He had only to ask and have. The Bishop of Liege was allowed for twenty-seven years to go on without taking orders at all, though he was bound by oath to his chapter to do so. We ask why was this allowed? He was brother of the Count of Geldern, an important recruit. All manner of 'irregularities', that is, slaughterings, plunderings, and burnings, were pardoned in Papalist clerics. For them, the rule against 'priests' brats' in orders had no terrors. Any one who would serve against Conrad [*Frederick's son—Ed.*], who was befriended by some leading Papalist, who was powerful enough to be worth winning over, found no prohibited degrees to any marriage, no cause or impediment to any match. If the keeping of an oath 'would redound to the disadvantage of the cause of the Church', absolution was openly given on this ground, or to reward an adherent or retain a waverer. Other supporters were secured by the simplest of all considerations, cash down . . . whatever is expedient, is lawful; oaths and vows, indulgences and absolutions and dispensations, benefices and tithes, Heaven itself and Hell, are all converted into the sinews of war. The cause sanctifies all that is done for it. Canonical rules, moral principles, legal sanctions, all go by the board and are cut adrift when 'St. Peter's bark is tossing in the storm'. . . .

It is not easy for a man of affairs to be a man of general culture too. But there is one study at least of which he must feel the value, the study of law. Sinibald Fieschi was already famous for his knowledge of this subject, when he first attracted the notice of Honorius III in 1223, and made himself useful to the Legate Ugolino. As Pope he always had about him in his palace a school of theology and of canon law. Among canonist Popes he ranks with Alexander III and Innocent III. Beyond this his intellectual interests did not go. He does not seem to have touched at any point the literature or art of his age. . . . His mind was severely concentrated on his one absorbing object. In this respect, as in so many others, he presents an utter contrast to Frederick II, that extraordinarily varied and many-sided personality, which reflected every aspect of his time and responded to every impulse, which embodied every form of culture, was full of the joy of life, of art, of friendship, and which presents to us a nature that if it sometimes repels, more often attracts, and is always full of a strange fascination; a nature so powerful, rich, and manifold, that by contrast with it the figure of the Pope is cold, narrow, unlovable, even inhuman. Yet at bottom they have qualities in common. In each there is the same swift clear intelligence, the same power of dominating and dwarfing those about them, the same matter-of-fact appeal to men's interests, the same infinite power of taking pains. Both have boundless patience, boundless confidence and resourcefulness. Each has one great purpose, and each is willing to advance towards it inch by inch, to sacrifice for it repose and health, and life itself. Frederick's belief in his destiny, in his imperial vocation to curb and rule Italy, is conspicuous. But Innocent had as strong a belief in the supremacy of the Holy See, and in its predestined triumph. 'The victory must needs come to the Church always.' This is what sustained him, so that hope radiated from him as from a pillar of fire when hope had gone out from all the rest. . . . 'Victory must needs come to the Church.' But had the Church really won? Was the victory of Innocent IV a victory for the Church? Was it even a victory for his own plans? He had taken the Church at her highest and best, in the climax of the thirteenth century, that glorious flowering-time of the Middle Ages, and in eleven years had destroyed half her power for good, and had launched her irretrievably upon a downward course. He had crushed the greatest ruling dynasty since the Caesars, and ruined the greatest attempt at government since the fall of Rome. In ruining the Empire, he had ruined also the future of the Papacy. Was this a victory?

Dante puts in the black starless air of the outer circle of the Inferno the shade of him *che fece lo gran rifiuto.** Of all Dante's tremendous verdicts, none has such a bitter ring of scorn as this. It is generally interpreted of one individual Pope; but it might well stand as judgement on the whole Papacy of the thirteenth century, when it bartered spiritual leadership for temporal rule, the legacy of St. Peter for the fatal dower of Constantine.

---

*[*Celestine V, who "made the great refusal" by abdicating from the papacy in* 1294—Ed.]